THE TWELVE CAESARS

VOLUME THREE OF THREE

GRAND TYPE

GRANDTYPECLASSICS.COM

The Twelve Caesars

Tranquillus, Gaius Suetonius c.69 – after c.122
Thomson, Alexander 1767 – 1801

Text edits © 2025 Grand Type Classics
Design © 2025 Grand Type Classics

Text set in 18 point Helvetica.
Chapter headings set in Helvetica Neue.

ISBN: 978-1-83412-386-8 Volume One
ISBN: 978-1-83412-387-5 Volume Two
ISBN: 978-1-83412-388-2 Volume Three

THE TWELVE CAESARS

VOLUME THREE OF THREE

To which are added,
His Lives of the Grammarians,
Rhetoricians, And Poets.

GAIUS SUETONIUS TRANQUILLUS

Translated by
Alexander Thomson, M.D.

GRAND TYPE CLASSICS

CONTENTS

The Twelve Caesars

VOLUME ONE

Preface   **7**

1 Caius Julius Casar   **13**
2 D. Octavius Caesar Augustus   **193**

VOLUME TWO

3 Tiberius Nero Caesar   **519**
4 Caius Caesar Caligula   **669**
5 Tiberius Claudius Drusus
Caesar   **779**
6 Nero Claudius Caesar   **886**

VOLUME THREE

7 Sergius Sulpicius Galba   **1050**
8 A. Salvius Otho   **1090**

9   Aulus Vitellius   **1118**
10   T. Flavius Vespasianus
     Augustus   **1153**
11   Titus Flavius Vespasianus
     Augustus   **1215**
12   Titus Flavius Domitianus   **1252**

Lives of Eminent Grammarians   **1322**

Lives of Eminent Rhetoricians   **1367**

Lives of the Poets
     The Life of Terence   **1383**
     The Life of Juvenal   **1398**
     The Life of Persius   **1402**
     The Life of Horace   **1409**
     The Life of Pliny   **1422**

SEVEN

Sergius Sulpicius Galba

I. THE RACE OF THE Caesars became extinct in Nero; an event prognosticated by various signs, two of which were particularly significant. Formerly, when Livia, after her marriage with Augustus, was making a visit to her villa at Veii[1], an eagle flying by, let drop upon her lap a

---

1 Veii; see the note, NERO, c. xxxix.

hen, with a sprig of laurel in her mouth, just as she had seized it. Livia gave orders to have the hen taken care of, and the sprig of laurel set; and the hen reared such a numerous brood of chickens, that the villa, to this day, is called the Villa of the Hens[2]. The laurel groves flourished so much, that the Caesars procured thence the boughs

---

2   The conventional term for what is most commonly known as,

"The Laurel, meed of mighty conquerors,
And poets sage,"–Spenser's Faerie Queen.

is retained throughout the translation. But the tree or shrub which had this distinction among the ancients, the Laurus nobilis of botany, the Daphne of the Greeks, is the bay-tree, indigenous in Italy, Greece, and the East, and introduced into England about 1562. Our laurel is a plant of a very different tribe, the Prunes lauro-cerasus, a native of the Levant and the Crimea, acclimated in England at a later period than the bay.

and crowns they bore at their triumphs. It was also their constant custom to plant others on the same spot, immediately after a triumph; and it was observed that, a little before the death of each prince, the tree which had been set by him died away. But in the last year of Nero, the whole plantation of laurels perished to the very roots, and the hens all died. About the same time, the temple of the Caesars[3] being struck with lightning, the heads of all the statues in it fell off at once; and Augustus's sceptre was dashed from his hands.

II. Nero was succeeded by Galba[4], who was not in the remotest degree allied to the family of the Caesars, but, without doubt, of very noble extraction, being descended

---

3   The Temple of the Caesars is generally supposed to be that dedicated by Julius Caesar to Venus genitrix, from whom the Julian family pretended to derive their descent. See JULIUS, c. lxi.; AUGUSTUS, c. ci.

4   A.U.C. 821.

from a great and ancient family; for he always used to put amongst his other titles, upon the bases of his statues, his being great-grandson to Q. Catulus Capitolinus. And when he came to be emperor, he set up the images of his ancestors in the hall[5] of the palace; according to the inscriptions on which, he carried up his pedigree on the

---

5   The Atrium, or Aula, was the court or hall of a house, the entrance to which was by the principal door. It appears to have been a large oblong square, surrounded with covered or arched galleries. Three sides of the Atrium were supported by pillars, which, in later times, were marble. The side opposite to the gate was called Tablinum; and the other two sides, Alae. The Tablinum contained books, and the records of what each member of the family had done in his magistracy. In the Atrium the nuptial couch was erected; and here the mistress of the family, with her maid-servants, wrought at spinning and weaving, which, in the time of the ancient Romans, was their principal employment.

father's side to Jupiter; and by the mother's to Pasiphae, the wife of Minos.

III. To give even a short account of the whole family, would be tedious. I shall, therefore, only slightly notice that branch of it from which he was descended. Why, or whence, the first of the Sulpicii who had the cognomen of Galba, was so called, is uncertain. Some are of opinion, that it was because he set fire to a city in Spain, after he had a long time attacked it to no purpose, with torches dipped in the gum called Galbanum: others said he was so named, because, in a lingering disease, he made use of it as a remedy, wrapped up in wool: others, on account of his being prodigiously corpulent, such a one being called, in the language of the Gauls, Galba; or, on the contrary, because he was of a slender habit of body, like those insects which breed in a sort of oak, and are called Galbae. Sergius Galba, a person of consular rank[6], and the most eloquent man of his time, gave a lustre to the family. History relates, that, when he was pro-praetor of Spain, he perfidiously put to the sword thirty thousand Lusitanians, and by that means gave occasion to the war of Viriatus[7]. His grandson being incensed against Julius Caesar, whose lieutenant he had been in Gaul, because he was through him disappointed of the consulship[8], joined with Cassius and Brutus in the conspiracy against him, for which he was condemned by the Pedian law. From him were descended the grandfather and father of the emperor Galba. The grandfather was more celebrated for his application to study, than for any figure he made in the government. For he rose no higher than the praetorship, but published a large and not

---

6   He was consul with L. Aurelius Cotta, A.U.C. 610.

7   A.U.C. 604.

8   A.U.C. 710.

uninteresting history. His father attained
to the consulship[9]: he was a short man
and hump-backed, but a tolerable orator,
and an industrious pleader. He was twice
married: the first of his wives was Mummia
Achaica, daughter of Catulus, and great-
grand-daughter of Lucius Mummius, who
sacked Corinth[10]; and the other, Livia
Ocellina, a very rich and beautiful woman,
by whom it is supposed he was courted for
the nobleness of his descent. They say, that
she was farther encouraged to persevere
in her advances, by an incident which
evinced the great ingenuousness of his
disposition. Upon her pressing her suit, he
took an opportunity, when they were alone,
of stripping off his toga, and showing her the
deformity of his person, that he might not
be thought to impose upon her. He had by
Achaica two sons, Caius and Sergius. The

---

9   A.U.C 775.
10   A.U.C. 608.

elder of these, Caius[11], having very much reduced his estate, retired from town, and being prohibited by Tiberius from standing for a pro-consulship in his year, put an end to his own life.

IV. The emperor Sergius Galba was born in the consulship of M. Valerius Messala, and Cn. Lentulus, upon the ninth of the calends of January [24th December][12], in a villa standing upon a hill, near Terracina, on the left-hand side of the road to Fundi[13]. Being adopted by his step-mother[14], he assumed the name of Livius, with the cognomen of Ocella, and changed his praenomen; for he afterwards used that of Lucius, instead of Sergius, until he arrived at the imperial dignity. It is well

---

11   Caius Sulpicius Galba, the emperor's brother, had been consul A.U.C. 774.
12   A.U.C. 751.
13   Now Fondi, which, with Terracina, still bearing its original name, lie on the road to Naples. See TIBERIUS, cc. v. and xxxix.
14   Livia Ocellina, mentioned just before.

known, that when he came once, amongst other boys of his own age, to pay his respects to Augustus, the latter, pinching his cheek, said to him, "And thou, child, too, wilt taste our imperial dignity." Tiberius, likewise, being told that he would come to be emperor, but at an advanced age, exclaimed, "Let him live, then, since that does not concern me!" When his grandfather was offering sacrifice to avert some ill omen from lightning, the entrails of the victim were snatched out of his hand by an eagle, and carried off into an oak-tree loaded with acorns. Upon this, the soothsayers said, that the family would come to be masters of the empire, but not until many years had elapsed: at which he, smiling, said, "Ay, when a mule comes to bear a foal." When Galba first declared against Nero, nothing gave him so much confidence of success, as a mule's happening at that time to have a foal. And whilst all others were shocked at the occurrence, as a most inauspicious prodigy, he alone regarded it as a most fortunate omen, calling to mind the sacrifice and saying of his grandfather. When he took upon him the manly habit, he dreamt that the goddess Fortune said to him, "I stand before your door weary; and unless I am speedily admitted, I shall fall into the hands of the first who comes to seize me." On his awaking, when the door of the house was opened, he found a brazen statue of the goddess, above a cubit long, close to the threshold, which he carried with slim to Tusculum, where he used to pass the summer season; and having consecrated it in an apartment of his house, he ever after worshipped it with a monthly sacrifice, and an anniversary vigil. Though but a very young man, he kept up an ancient but obsolete custom, and now nowhere observed, except in his own family, which was, to have his freedmen and slaves appear in a body before him twice a day, morning and evening, to offer him their salutations.

V. Amongst other liberal studies, he applied

himself to the law. He married Lepida[15], by whom he had two sons; but the mother and children all dying, he continued a widower; nor could he be prevailed upon to marry again, not even Agrippina herself, at that time left a widow by the death of Domitius, who had employed all her blandishments to allure him to her embraces, while he was a married man; insomuch that Lepida's mother, when in company with several married women, rebuked her for it, and even went so far as to cuff her. Most of all, he courted the empress Livia[16], by whose favour, while she was living, he made a considerable figure, and narrowly missed being enriched by the will which she left at her death; in which she distinguished him from the rest of the legatees, by a legacy of fifty millions of sesterces. But because the sum was expressed in figures, and not in words at length, it was reduced by her heir, Tiberius, to five hundred thousand: and even

---

15   A.U.C. 751.
16   The widow of the emperor Augustus.

this he never received.[17]

VI. Filling the great offices before the age required for it by law, during his praetorship, at the celebration of games in honour of the goddess Flora, he presented the new spectacle of elephants walking upon ropes. He was then governor of the province of Aquitania for near a year, and soon afterwards took the consulship in the usual course, and held it for six months[18]. It so happened that he succeeded L. Domitius, the father of Nero, and was succeeded by Salvius Otho, father to the emperor of that name; so that his holding it between

---

17   Suetonius seems to have forgotten, that, according to his own testimony, this legacy, as well as those left by Tiberius, was paid by Caligula. "Legata ex testamento Tiberii; quamquam abolito, sed et Juliae Augustae, quod Tiberius suppresserat, cum fide, ac sine calumnia repraesentate persolvit." CALIG. c. xvi.

18   A.U.C. 786.

the sons of these two men, looked like a presage of his future advancement to the empire. Being appointed by Caius Caesar to supersede Gaetulicus in his command, the day after his joining the legions, he put a stop to their plaudits in a public spectacle, by issuing an order, "That they should keep their hands under their cloaks." Immediately upon which, the following verse became very common in the camp:

Disce, miles, militare: Galba est, non Gaetulicus.
Learn, soldier, now in arms to use your hands,
'Tis Galba, not Gaetulicus, commands.

With equal strictness, he would allow of no petitions for leave of absence from the camp. He hardened the soldiers, both old and young, by constant exercise; and having quickly reduced within their own limits the barbarians who had made inroads into Gaul, upon Caius's coming into Germany, he so far recommended himself and his army to that emperor's approbation, that, amongst the innumerable troops drawn from all the provinces of the empire, none met with higher commendation, or greater rewards from him. He likewise distinguished himself by heading an escort, with a shield in his hand[19], and running at the side of the emperor's chariot twenty miles together.

VII. Upon the news of Caius's death, though many earnestly pressed him to lay hold of that opportunity of seizing the empire, he chose rather to be quiet. On this account, he was in great favour with Claudius, and being received into the number of his friends, stood so high in his good opinion, that the expedition to Britain[20] was for

---

19   "Scuto moderatus;" another reading in the parallel passage of Tacitus is scuto immodice oneratus, burdened with the heavy weight of a shield.

20   It would appear that Galba was to have

some time suspended, because he was suddenly seized with a slight indisposition. He governed Africa, as pro-consul, for two years; being chosen out of the regular course to restore order in the province, which was in great disorder from civil dissensions, and the alarms of the barbarians. His administration was distinguished by great strictness and equity, even in matters of small importance. A soldier upon some expedition being charged with selling, in a great scarcity of corn, a bushel of wheat, which was all he had left, for a hundred denarii, he forbad him to be relieved by any body, when he came to be in want himself; and accordingly he died of famine. When sitting in judgment, a cause being brought before him about some beast of burden, the ownership of which was claimed by two persons; the evidence being slight on both sides, and it being difficult to

---

accompanied Claudius in his expedition to Britain; which is related before, CLAUDIUS, c. xvii.

come at the truth, he ordered the beast to be led to a pond at which he had used to be watered, with his head muffled up, and the covering being there removed, that he should be the property of the person whom he followed of his own accord, after drinking.

VIII. For his achievements, both at this time in Africa, and formerly in Germany, he received the triumphal ornaments, and three sacerdotal appointments, one among The Fifteen, another in the college of Titius, and a third amongst the Augustals; and from that time to the middle of Nero's reign, he lived for the most part in retirement. He never went abroad so much as to take the air, without a carriage attending him, in which there was a million of sesterces in gold, ready at hand; until at last, at the time he was living in the town of Fundi, the province of Hispania Tarraconensis was offered him. After his arrival in the province, whilst he was sacrificing in a temple, a boy who attended with a censer, became all on a sudden grey-headed. This incident was regarded by some as a token of an approaching revolution in the government, and that an old man would succeed a young one: that is, that he would succeed Nero. And not long after, a thunderbolt falling into a lake in Cantabria[21], twelve axes were found in it; a manifest sign of the supreme power.

IX. He governed the province during eight years, his administration being of an uncertain and capricious character. At first he was active, vigorous, and indeed excessively severe, in the punishment of offenders. For, a money-dealer having committed some fraud in the way of his business, he cut off his hands, and nailed them to his counter. Another, who had poisoned an orphan, to whom he was guardian, and next heir to the estate, he crucified. On this delinquent

---

21   It has been remarked before, that the Cantabria of the ancients is now the province of Biscay.

imploring the protection of the law, and crying out that he was a Roman citizen, he affected to afford him some alleviation, and to mitigate his punishment, by a mark of honour, ordered a cross, higher than usual, and painted white, to be erected for him. But by degrees he gave himself up to a life of indolence and inactivity, from the fear of giving Nero any occasion of jealousy, and because, as he used to say, "Nobody was obliged to render an account of their leisure hours." He was holding a court of justice on the circuit at New Carthage[22], when he received intelligence of the insurrection in Gaul[23]; and while the lieutenant of Aquitania was soliciting his assistance, letters were brought from Vindex, requesting him "to assert the rights of mankind, and put himself at their head to relieve them from the tyranny of Nero." Without any long demur, he accepted the invitation, from a mixture

---

22   Now Carthagena.
23   A.U.C. 821.

of fear and hope. For he had discovered that private orders had been sent by Nero to his procurators in the province to get him dispatched; and he was encouraged to the enterprise, as well by several auspices and omens, as by the prophecy of a young woman of good, family. The more so, because the priest of Jupiter at Clunia[24], admonished by a dream, had discovered in the recesses of the temple some verses similar to those in which she had delivered her prophecy. These had also been uttered by a girl under divine inspiration, about two hundred years before. The import of the verses was, "That in time, Spain should give the world a lord and master."

X. Taking his seat on the tribunal, therefore, as if there was no other business than the manumitting of slaves, he had the effigies of a number of persons who had been condemned and put to death by Nero, set

---

24   Now Corunna.

up before him, whilst a noble youth stood by, who had been banished, and whom he had purposely sent for from one of the neighbouring Balearic isles; and lamenting the condition of the times, and being thereupon unanimously saluted by the title of Emperor, he publicly declared himself "only the lieutenant of the senate and people of Rome." Then shutting the courts, he levied legions and auxiliary troops among the provincials, besides his veteran army consisting of one legion, two wings of horse, and three cohorts. Out of the military leaders most distinguished for age and prudence, he formed a kind of senate, with whom to advise upon all matters of importance, as often as occasion should require. He likewise chose several young men of the equestrian order, who were to be allowed the privilege of wearing the gold ring, and, being called "The Reserve," should mount guard before his bed-chamber, instead of the legionary soldiers. He likewise issued proclamations throughout the provinces of the empire, exhorting all to rise in arms unanimously, and aid the common cause, by all the ways and means in their power. About the same time, in fortifying a town, which he had pitched upon for a military post, a ring was found, of antique workmanship, in the stone of which was engraved the goddess Victory with a trophy. Presently after, a ship of Alexandria arrived at Dertosa[25], loaded with arms, without any person to steer it, or so much as a single sailor or passenger on board. From this incident, nobody entertained the least doubt but the war upon which they were entering was just and honourable, and favoured likewise by the gods; when all on a sudden the whole design was exposed to failure. One of the two wings of horse, repenting of the violation of their oath to Nero, attempted to desert him upon his approach to the camp, and

---

25   Tortosa, on the Ebro.

were with some difficulty kept in their duty. And some slaves who had been presented to him by a freedman of Nero's, on purpose to murder him, had like to have killed him as he went through a narrow passage to the bath. Being overheard to encourage one another not to lose the opportunity, they were called to an account concerning it; and recourse being had to the torture, a confession was extorted from them.

XI. These dangers were followed by the death of Vindex, at which being extremely discouraged, as if fortune had quite forsaken him, he had thoughts of putting an end to his own life; but receiving advice by his messengers from Rome that Nero was slain, and that all had taken an oath to him as emperor, he laid aside the title of lieutenant, and took upon him that of Caesar. Putting himself upon his march in his general's cloak, and a dagger hanging from his neck before his breast, he did not resume the use of the toga, until Nymphidius

Sabinus, prefect of the pretorian guards at Rome, with the two lieutenants, Fonteius Capito in Germany, and Claudius Macer in Africa, who opposed his advancement, were all put down.

XII. Rumours of his cruelty and avarice had reached the city before his arrival; such as that he had punished some cities of Spain and Gaul, for not joining him readily, by the imposition of heavy taxes, and some by levelling their walls; and had put to death the governors and procurators with their wives and children: likewise that a golden crown, of fifteen pounds weight, taken out of the temple of Jupiter, with which he was presented by the people of Tarracona, he had melted down, and had exacted from them three ounces which were wanting in the weight. This report of him was confirmed and increased, as soon as he entered the town. For some seamen who had been taken from the fleet, and enlisted among the troops by Nero, he obliged to return to their former condition; but they refusing to comply, and obstinately clinging to the more honourable service under their eagles and standards, he not only dispersed them by a body of horse, but likewise decimated them. He also disbanded a cohort of Germans, which had been formed by the preceding emperors, for their body-guard, and upon many occasions found very faithful; and sent them back into their own country, without giving them any gratuity, pretending that they were more inclined to favour the advancement of Cneius Dolabella, near whose gardens they encamped, than his own. The following ridiculous stories were also related of him; but whether with or without foundation, I know not; such as, that when a more sumptuous entertainment than usual was served up, he fetched a deep groan: that when one of the stewards presented him with an account of his expenses, he reached him a dish of legumes from his table as a reward for his care and diligence; and when Canus, the piper, had played much to his satisfaction, he presented him, with his own hand, five denarii taken out of his pocket.

XIII. His arrival, therefore, in town was not very agreeable to the people; and this appeared at the next public spectacle. For when the actors in a farce began a well-known song,

Venit, io, Simus[26] a villa:
Lo! Clodpate from his village comes;

all the spectators, with one voice, went on with the rest, repeating and acting the first verse several times over.

XIV. He possessed himself of the imperial power with more favour and authority than he administered it, although he gave many

---

26   "Simus," literally, flat-nosed, was a cant word, used for a clown; Galba being jeered for his rusticity, in consequence of his long retirement. See c. viii. Indeed, they called Spain his farm.

proofs of his being an excellent prince: but these were not so grateful to the people, as his misconduct was offensive. He was governed by three favourites, who, because they lived in the palace, and were constantly about him, obtained the name of his pedagogues. These were Titus Vinius, who had been his lieutenant in Spain, a man of insatiable avarice; Cornelius Laco, who, from an assessor to the prince, was advanced to be prefect of the pretorian guards, a person of intolerable arrogance, as well as indolence; and his freedman Icelus, dignified a little before with the privilege of wearing the gold ring, and the use of the cognomen Martianus, who became a candidate for the highest honour within the reach of any person of the equestrian order[27]. He resigned himself so implicitly into the power of those three favourites, who governed in every thing

---

27   The command of the pretorian guards.

according to the capricious impulse of their vices and tempers, and his authority was so much abused by them, that the tenor of his conduct was not very consistent with itself. At one time, he was more rigorous and frugal, at another, more lavish and negligent, than became a prince who had been chosen by the people, and was so far advanced in years. He condemned some men of the first rank in the senatorian and equestrian orders, upon a very slight suspicion, and without trial. He rarely granted the freedom of the city to any one; and the privilege belonging to such as had three children, only to one or two; and that with great difficulty, and only for a limited time. When the judges petitioned to have a sixth decury added to their number, he not only denied them, but abolished the vacation which had been granted them by Claudius for the winter, and the beginning of the year.

XV. It was thought that he likewise intended

to reduce the offices held by senators and men of the equestrian order, to a term of two years' continuance; and to bestow them only on those who were unwilling to accept them, and had refused them. All the grants of Nero he recalled, saving only the tenth part of them. For this purpose he gave a commission to fifty Roman knights; with orders, that if players or wrestlers had sold what had been formerly given them, it should be exacted from the purchasers, since the others, having, no doubt, spent the money, were not in a condition to pay. But on the other hand, he suffered his attendants and freedmen to sell or give away the revenue of the state, or immunities from taxes, and to punish the innocent, or pardon criminals, at pleasure. Nay, when the Roman people were very clamorous for the punishment of Halotus and Tigellinus, two of the most mischievous amongst all the emissaries of Nero, he protected them, and even bestowed on Halotus one of the best procurations in his disposal. And as to Tigellinus, he even reprimanded the people for their cruelty by a proclamation.

XVI. By this conduct, he incurred the hatred of all orders of the people, but especially of the soldiery. For their commanders having promised them in his name a donative larger than usual, upon their taking the oath to him before his arrival at Rome; he refused to make it good, frequently bragging, "that it was his custom to choose his soldiers, not buy them." Thus the troops became exasperated against him in all quarters. The pretorian guards he alarmed with apprehensions of danger and unworthy treatment; disbanding many of them occasionally as disaffected to his government, and favourers of Nymphidius. But most of all, the army in Upper Germany was incensed against him, as being defrauded of the rewards due to them for the service they had rendered in the insurrection of the Gauls under Vindex. They were, therefore, the first who ventured to break into open mutiny, refusing upon the calends [the 1st] of January, to take any oath of allegiance, except to the senate; and they immediately dispatched deputies to the pretorian troops, to let them know, "they did not like the emperor who had been set up in Spain," and to desire that "they would make choice of another, who might meet with the approbation of all the armies."

XVII. Upon receiving intelligence of this, imagining that he was slighted not so much on account of his age, as for having no children, he immediately singled out of a company of young persons of rank, who came to pay their compliments to him, Piso Frugi Licinianus, a youth of noble descent and great talents, for whom he had before contracted such a regard, that he had appointed him in his will the heir both of his estate and name. Him he now styled his son, and taking him to the camp, adopted him in the presence of the assembled troops, but without making any mention of a donative. This circumstance afforded the better opportunity to Marcus Salvius Otho of accomplishing his object, six days after the adoption.

XVIII. Many remarkable prodigies had happened from the very beginning of his reign, which forewarned him of his approaching fate. In every town through which he passed in his way from Spain to Rome, victims were slain on the right and left of the roads; and one of these, which was a bull, being maddened with the stroke of the axe, broke the rope with which it was tied, and running straight against his chariot, with his fore-feet elevated, bespattered him with blood. Likewise, as he was alighting, one of the guard, being pushed forward by the crowd, had very nearly wounded him with his lance. And upon his entering the city and, afterwards, the palace, he was welcomed with an earthquake, and a noise like the bellowing of cattle. These signs of ill-fortune were followed by some that were still more apparently such. Out of all his treasures he had selected a necklace of pearls and jewels, to adorn his statue of Fortune at Tusculum. But it suddenly occurring to him that it deserved a more august place, he consecrated it to the Capitoline Venus; and next night, he dreamt that Fortune appeared to him, complaining that she had been defrauded of the present intended her, and threatening to resume what she had given him. Terrified at this denunciation, at break of day he sent forward some persons to Tusculum, to make preparations for a sacrifice which might avert the displeasure of the goddess; and when he himself arrived at the place, he found nothing but some hot embers upon the altar, and an old man in black standing by, holding a little incense in a glass, and some wine in an earthern pot. It was remarked, too, that whilst he was sacrificing upon the calends of January, the chaplet fell from his head, and upon his consulting the pullets for omens, they flew away. Farther, upon the day of his adopting Piso, when he was to harangue the soldiers, the seat which he used upon those occasions, through the neglect of his attendants, was not placed, according to custom, upon his tribunal; and in the senate-house, his curule chair was set with the back forward.

XIX. The day before he was slain, as he was sacrificing in the morning, the augur warned him from time to time to be upon his guard, for that he was in danger from assassins, and that they were near at hand. Soon after, he was informed, that Otho was in possession of the pretorian camp. And though most of his friends advised him to repair thither immediately, in hopes that he might quell the tumult by his authority and presence, he resolved to do nothing more than keep close within the palace, and secure himself by guards of the legionary soldiers, who were quartered in different parts about the city. He put on a linen coat of mail, however, remarking at the same time, that it would avail him little against the points of so many swords. But being tempted out by false reports, which the conspirators had purposely spread to induce him to venture abroad–some few of those about him too hastily assuring him that the tumult had ceased, the mutineers were apprehended, and the rest coming to congratulate him, resolved to continue firm in their obedience–he went forward to meet them with so much confidence, that upon a soldier's boasting that he had killed Otho, he asked him, "By what authority?" and proceeded as far as the Forum. There the knights, appointed to dispatch him, making their way through the crowd of citizens, upon seeing him at a distance, halted a while; after which, galloping up to him, now abandoned by all his attendants, they put him to death.

XX. Some authors relate, that upon their

first approach he cried out, "What do you mean, fellow-soldiers? I am yours, and you are mine," and promised them a donative: but the generality of writers relate, that he offered his throat to them, saying, "Do your work, and strike, since you are resolved upon it." It is remarkable, that not one of those who were at hand, ever made any attempt to assist the emperor; and all who were sent for, disregarded the summons, except a troop of Germans. They, in consideration of his late kindness in showing them particular attention during a sickness which prevailed in the camp, flew to his aid, but came too late; for, being not well acquainted with the town, they had taken a circuitous route. He was slain near the Curtian Lake[28], and there left, until a common soldier returning from the receipt of his allowance of corn, throwing down the load which he carried, cut off his head.

---

28   In the Forum. See AUGUSTUS, c. lvii.

There being upon it no hair, by which he might hold it, he hid it in the bosom of his dress; but afterwards thrusting his thumb into the mouth, he carried it in that manner to Otho, who gave it to the drudges and slaves who attended the soldiers; and they, fixing it upon the point of a spear, carried it in derision round the camp, crying out as they went along, "You take your fill of joy in your old age." They were irritated to this pitch of rude banter, by a report spread a few days before, that, upon some one's commending his person as still florid and vigorous, he replied,

Eti moi menos empedoi estin.[29]
My strength, as yet, has suffered no decay.

A freedman of Petrobius's, who himself had belonged to Nero's family, purchased

---

29   II. v. 254.

the head from them at the price of a hundred gold pieces, and threw it into the place where, by Galba's order, his patron had been put to death. At last, after some time, his steward Argius buried it, with the rest of his body, in his own gardens near the Aurelian Way.

XXI. In person he was of a good size, bald before, with blue eyes, and an aquiline nose; and his hands and feet were so distorted with the gout, that he could neither wear a shoe, nor turn over the leaves of a book, or so much as hold it. He had likewise an excrescence in his right side, which hung down to that degree, that it was with difficulty kept up by a bandage.

XXII. He is reported to have been a great eater, and usually took his breakfast in the winter-time before day. At supper, he fed very heartily, giving the fragments which were left, by handfuls, to be distributed amongst the attendants. In his lust, he was more inclined to the male sex, and such of them too as were old. It is said of him, that in Spain, when Icelus, an old catamite of his, brought him the news of Nero's death, he not only kissed him lovingly before company, but begged of him to remove all impediments, and then took him aside into a private apartment.

XXIII. He perished in the seventy-third year of his age, and the seventh month of his reign[30]. The senate, as soon as they could with safety, ordered a statue to be erected for him upon the naval column, in that part of the Forum where he was slain. But Vespasian cancelled the decree, upon a suspicion that he had sent assassins from Spain into Judaea to murder him.

* * * * * *

GALBA was, for a private man, the most wealthy of any who had ever aspired to the imperial dignity. He valued himself upon

_____

30   A.U.C. 822.

his being descended from the family of the Servii, but still more upon his relation to Quintus Catulus Capitolinus, celebrated for integrity and virtue. He was likewise distantly related to Livia, the wife of Augustus; by whose interest he was preferred from the station which he held in the palace, to the dignity of consul; and who left him a great legacy at her death. His parsimonious way of living, and his aversion to all superfluity or excess, were construed into avarice as soon as he became emperor; whence Plutarch observes, that the pride which he took in his temperance and economy was unseasonable. While he endeavoured to reform the profusion in the public expenditure, which prevailed in the reign of Nero, he ran into the opposite extreme; and it is objected to him by some historians, that he maintained not the imperial dignity in a degree consistent even with decency. He was not sufficiently attentive either to his own security or the tranquillity of the state, when he refused to pay the soldiers the donative which he had promised them. This breach of faith seems to be the only act in his life that affects his integrity; and it contributed more to his ruin than even the odium which he incurred by the open venality and rapaciousness of his favourites, particularly Vinius.

EIGHT

A. Salvius Otho

I. THE ANCESTORS OF OTHO were originally of the town of Ferentum, of an ancient and honourable family, and, indeed, one of the most considerable in Etruria. His grandfather, M. Salvius Otho (whose father was a Roman knight, but his mother of mean extraction, for it is not certain whether she was free-born), by the favour of Livia Augusta, in whose house he had his education, was made a senator, but never rose higher than the praetorship. His father, Lucius Otho, was by the mother's side nobly descended, allied to several great families, and so dearly beloved by Tiberius, and so much resembled him in his features, that most people believed Tiberius was his father. He behaved with great strictness and severity, not only in the city offices, but in the pro-consulship of Africa, and some extraordinary commands in the army. He had the courage to punish with death some soldiers in Illyricum, who, in the disturbance attempted by Camillus, upon changing their minds, had put their generals to the sword, as promoters of that insurrection against Claudius. He ordered the execution to take place in the front of the camp[31], and under

---

31   On the esplanade, where the standards, objects of religious reverence, were planted. See note to c. vi. Criminals were usually executed outside the Vallum, and in the presence of a centurion.

his own eyes; though he knew they had been advanced to higher ranks in the army by Claudius, on that very account. By this action he acquired fame, but lessened his favour at court; which, however, he soon recovered, by discovering to Claudius a design upon his life, carried on by a Roman knight[32], and which he had learnt from some of his slaves. For the senate ordered a statue of him to be erected in the palace; an honour which had been conferred but upon very few before him. And Claudius advanced him to the dignity of a patrician, commending him, at the same time, in the highest terms, and concluding with these words: "A man, than whom I don't so much as wish to have children that should be better." He had two sons by a very noble woman, Albia Terentia, namely; Lucius Titianus, and a younger called Marcus, who had the same cognomen as himself. He

---

32   Probably one of the two mentioned in CLAUDIUS, c. xiii.

had also a daughter, whom he contracted to Drusus, Germanicus's son, before she was of marriageable age.

II. The emperor Otho was born upon the fourth of the calends of May [28th April], in the consulship of Camillus Aruntius and Domitius Aenobarbus[33]. He was from his earliest youth so riotous and wild, that he was often severely scourged by his father. He was said to run about in the night-time, and seize upon any one he met, who was either drunk or too feeble to make resistance, and toss him in a blanket[34]. After his father's death, to make his court the more effectually to a freedwoman about the palace, who was in great favour, he pretended to be in love with her, though she was old, and almost decrepit. Having by her means got into Nero's good graces, he soon became one of the principal favourites, by the congeniality

33   A.U.C. 784 or 785.
34   "Distento sago impositum in sublime jactare."

of his disposition to that of the emperor or, as some say, by the reciprocal practice of mutual pollution. He had so great a sway at court, that when a man of consular rank was condemned for bribery, having tampered with him for a large sum of money, to procure his pardon; before he had quite effected it, he scrupled not to introduce him into the senate, to return his thanks.

III. Having, by means of this woman, insinuated himself into all the emperor's secrets, he, upon the day designed for the murder of his mother, entertained them both at a very splendid feast, to prevent suspicion. Poppaea Sabina, for whom Nero entertained such a violent passion that he had taken her from her husband[35] and entrusted her to him, he received, and went through the form of marrying her. And not satisfied with obtaining her favours, he loved her so extravagantly, that he could

---

35   See NERO, c. xxxv.

not with patience bear Nero for his rival. It is certainly believed that he not only refused admittance to those who were sent by Nero to fetch her, but that, on one occasion, he shut him out, and kept him standing before the door, mixing prayers and menaces in vain, and demanding back again what was entrusted to his keeping. His pretended marriage, therefore, being dissolved, he was sent lieutenant into Lusitania. This treatment of him was thought sufficiently severe, because harsher proceedings might have brought the whole farce to light, which, notwithstanding, at last came out, and was published to the world in the following distich:–

Cur Otho mentitus sit, quaeritis, exul honore?
Uxoris moechus caeperat esse suae.
You ask why Otho's banish'd? Know, the cause

Comes not within the verge of vulgar laws.
Against all rules of fashionable life,
The rogue had dared to sleep with his own wife.

He governed the province in quality of quaestor for ten years, with singular moderation and justice.

IV. As soon as an opportunity of revenge offered, he readily joined in Galba's enterprises, and at the same time conceived hopes of obtaining the imperial dignity for himself. To this he was much encouraged by the state of the times, but still more by the assurances given him by Seleucus, the astrologer, who, having formerly told him that he would certainly out-live Nero, came to him at that juncture unexpectedly, promising him again that he should succeed to the empire, and that in a very short time. He, therefore, let slip no opportunity of making his court to every one about him by all manner of civilities. As often as he entertained Galba at supper, he distributed to every man of the cohort which attended the emperor on guard, a gold piece; endeavouring likewise to oblige the rest of the soldiers in one way or another. Being chosen an arbitrator by one who had a dispute with his neighbour about a piece of land, he bought it, and gave it him; so that now almost every body thought and said, that he was the only man worthy of succeeding to the empire.

V. He entertained hopes of being adopted by Galba, and expected it every day. But finding himself disappointed, by Piso's being preferred before him, he turned his thoughts to obtaining his purpose by the use of violence; and to this he was instigated, as well by the greatness of his debts, as by resentment at Galba's conduct towards him. For he did not conceal his conviction, "that he could not stand his ground unless he became emperor, and that it signified nothing whether he fell by the hands of his enemies in the field, or of his creditors in the Forum." He had a few days before squeezed out of one of the emperor's slaves a million of sesterces for procuring him a stewardship; and this was the whole fund he had for carrying on so great an enterprise. At first the design was entrusted to only five of the guard, but afterwards to ten others, each of the five naming two. They had every one ten thousand sesterces paid down, and were promised fifty thousand more. By these, others were drawn in, but not many; from a confident assurance, that when the matter came to the crisis, they should have enough to join them.

VI. His first intention was, immediately after the departure of Piso, to seize the camp, and fall upon Galba, whilst he was at supper in the palace; but he was restrained by a regard for the cohort at that time on duty, lest he should bring too great an odium upon it; because it happened that the same cohort was on guard before, both when Caius was slain, and Nero deserted. For some time afterwards, he was restrained also by scruples about the omens, and by the advice of Seleucus. Upon the day fixed at last for the enterprise, having given his accomplices notice to wait for him in the Forum near the temple of Saturn, at the gilded mile-stone[36], he went in the morning to pay his respects to Galba; and being received with a kiss as usual, he attended him at sacrifice, and heard the predictions of the augur[37]. A freedman of his, then

---

36   The Milliare Aureum was a pillar of stone set up at the top of the Forum, from which all the great military roads throughout Italy started, the distances to the principal towns being marked upon it. Dio (lib. liv.) says that it was erected by the emperor Augustus, when he was curator of the roads.

37   Haruspex, Auspex, or Augur, denoted any person who foretold futurity, or interpreted

bringing him word that the architects were come, which was the signal agreed upon, he withdrew, as if it were with a design to view a house upon sale, and went out by a back-door of the palace to the place appointed. Some say he pretended to be seized with an ague fit, and ordered those about him to make that excuse for him, if

---

omens. There was at Rome a body of priests, or college, under this title, whose office it was to foretell future events, chiefly from the flight, chirping, or feeding of birds, and from other appearances. They were of the greatest authority in the Roman state; for nothing of importance was done in public affairs, either at home or abroad, in peace or war, without consulting them. The Romans derived the practice of augury chiefly from the Tuscans; and anciently their youth used to be instructed as carefully in this art, as afterwards they were in the Greek literature. For this purpose, by a decree of the senate, a certain number of the sons of the leading men at Rome was sent to the twelve states of Etruria for instruction.

he was inquired after. Being then quickly concealed in a woman's litter, he made the best of his way for the camp. But the bearers growing tired, he got out, and began to run. His shoe becoming loose, he stopped again, but being immediately raised by his attendants upon their shoulders, and unanimously saluted by the title of EMPEROR, he came amidst auspicious acclamations and drawn swords into the Principia[38] in the camp; all who met him

---

38   See before, note, c. i. The Principia was a broad open space, which separated the lower part of the Roman camp from the upper, and extended the whole breadth of the camp. In this place was erected the tribunal of the general, when he either administered justice or harangued the army. Here likewise the tribunes held their courts, and punishments were inflicted. The principal standards of the army, as it has been already mentioned, were deposited in the Principia; and in it also stood the altars of the gods, and the images of the Emperors, by which the soldiers swore.

joining in the cavalcade, as if they had been privy to the design. Upon this, sending some soldiers to dispatch Galba and Piso, he said nothing else in his address to the soldiery, to secure their affections, than these few words: "I shall be content with whatever ye think fit to leave me."

VII. Towards the close of the day, he entered the senate, and after he had made a short speech to them, pretending that he had been seized in the streets, and compelled by violence to assume the imperial authority, which he designed to exercise in conjunction with them, he retired to the palace. Besides other compliments which he received from those who flocked about him to congratulate and flatter him, he was called Nero by the mob, and manifested no intention of declining that cognomen. Nay, some authors relate, that he used it in his official acts, and the first letters he sent to the governors of provinces. He suffered all his images and statues to be replaced, and restored his procurators and freedmen to their former posts. And the first writing which he signed as emperor, was a promise of fifty millions of sesterces to finish the Golden-house[39]. He is said to have been greatly frightened that night in his sleep, and to have groaned heavily; and being found, by those who came running in to see what the matter was, lying upon the floor before his bed, he endeavoured by every kind of atonement to appease the ghost of Galba, by which he had found himself violently tumbled out of bed. The next day, as he was taking the omens, a great storm arising, and sustaining a grievous fall, he muttered to himself from time to time:

Ti gar moi kai makrois aulois;[40]

---

39   See NERO, c. xxxi. The sum estimated as requisite for its completion amounted to 2,187,500 pounds of our money.

40   The two last words, literally translated,

A. Salvius Otho

What business have I the loud trumpets to sound!

VIII. About the same time, the armies in Germany took an oath to Vitellius as emperor. Upon receiving this intelligence, he advised the senate to send thither deputies, to inform them, that a prince had been already chosen; and to persuade them to peace and a good understanding. By letters and messages, however, he offered Vitellius to make him his colleague in the empire, and his son-in-law. But a war being now unavoidable, and the generals and troops sent forward by Vitellius, advancing, he had a proof of the attachment and fidelity of the pretorian guards, which had nearly proved fatal to the senatorian order. It had been judged proper that some arms should be given out of the

---

mean "long trumpets;" such as were used at sacrifices. The sense is, therefore, "What have I to do, my hands stained with blood, with performing religious ceremonies!"

stores, and conveyed to the fleet by the marine troops. While they were employed in fetching these from the camp in the night, some of the guards suspecting treachery, excited a tumult; and suddenly the whole body, without any of their officers at their head, ran to the palace, demanding that the entire senate should be put to the sword; and having repulsed some of the tribunes who endeavoured to stop them, and slain others, they broke, all bloody as they were, into the banquetting room, inquiring for the emperor; nor would they quit the place until they had seen him. He now entered upon his expedition against Vitellius with great alacrity, but too much precipitation, and without any regard to the ominous circumstances which attended it. For the Ancilia[41] had been taken out of the temple

---

41   The Ancile was a round shield, said to have fallen from heaven in the reign of Numa, and supposed to be the shield of Mars. It was kept with great care in the sanctuary of his

of Mars, for the usual procession, but were not yet replaced; during which interval it had of old been looked upon as very unfortunate to engage in any enterprise. He likewise set forward upon the day when the worshippers of the Mother of the gods[42] begin their lamentations and wailing. Besides these, other unlucky omens attended him. For, in

---

temple, as a symbol of the perpetuity of the Roman empire; and that it might not be stolen, eleven others were made exactly similar to it.

42   This ideal personage, who has been mentioned before, AUGUSTUS, c. lxviii., was the goddess Cybele, the wife of Saturn, called also Rhea, Ops, Vesta, Magna, Mater, etc. She was painted as a matron, crowned with towers, sitting in a chariot drawn by lions. A statue of her, brought from Pessinus in Phrygia to Rome, in the time of the second Punic war, was much honoured there. Her priests, called the Galli and Corybantes, were castrated; and worshipped her with the sound of drums, tabors, pipes, and cymbals. The rites of this goddess were disgraced by great indecencies.

a victim offered to Father Dis[43], he found the signs such as upon all other occasions are regarded as favourable; whereas, in that sacrifice, the contrary intimations are judged the most propitious. At his first setting forward, he was stopped by inundations of the Tiber; and at twenty miles' distance from the city, found the road blocked up by the fall of houses.

IX. Though it was the general opinion that it would be proper to protract the war, as the enemy were distressed by famine and the straitness of their quarters, yet he

---

43   Otherwise called Orcus, Pluto, Jupiter Infernus, and Stygnis. He was the brother of Jupiter, and king of the infernal regions. His wife was Proserpine, the daughter of Ceres, whom he carried off as she was gathering flowers in the plains of Enna, in Sicily. The victims offered to the infernal gods were black: they were killed with their faces bent downwards; the knife was applied from below, and the blood was poured into a ditch.

resolved with equal rashness to force them to an engagement as soon as possible; whether from impatience of prolonged anxiety, and in the hope of bringing matters to an issue before the arrival of Vitellius, or because he could not resist the ardour of the troops, who were all clamorous for battle. He was not, however, present at any of those which ensued, but stayed behind at Brixellum[44]. He had the advantage in three slight engagements, near the Alps, about Placentia, and a place called Castor's[45]; but was, by a fraudulent stratagem of the enemy, defeated in the last and greatest battle, at Bedriacum[46]. For, some hopes of

---

44   A town between Mantua and Cremona.

45   The temple of Castor. It stood about twelve miles from Cremona. Tacitus gives some details of this action. Hist. ii. 243.

46   Both Greek and Latin authors differ in the mode of spelling the name of this place, the first syllable being written Beb, Bet, and Bret. It is now a small village called Labino, between

a conference being given, and the soldiers being drawn up to hear the conditions of peace declared, very unexpectedly, and amidst their mutual salutations, they were obliged to stand to their arms. Immediately upon this he determined to put an end to his life, more, as many think, and not without reason, out of shame, at persisting in a struggle for the empire to the hazard of the public interest and so many lives, than from despair, or distrust of his troops. For he had still in reserve, and in full force, those whom he had kept about him for a second trial of his fortune, and others were coming up from Dalmatia, Pannonia, and Moesia; nor were the troops lately defeated so far discouraged as not to be ready, even of themselves, to run all risks in order to wipe off their recent disgrace.

X. My father, Suetonius Lenis[47], was in this

Cremona and Verona.

47   Lenis was a name of similar signification with that of Tranquillus, borne by his son,

the author of the present work. We find from Tacitus, that there was, among Otho's generals, in this battle, another person of the name of Suetonius, whose cognomen was Paulinus; with whom our author's father must not be confounded. Lenis was only a tribune of the thirteenth legion, the position of which in the battle is mentioned by Tacitus, Hist. xi. 24, and was angusticlavius, wearing only the narrow stripe, as not being of the senatorial order; while Paulinus was a general, commanding a legion, at least, and a consular man; having filled that Office A.U.C. 818. There seems no doubt that Suetonius Paulinus was the same general who distinguished himself by his successes and cruelties in Britain. NERO, c. xviii., and note.] Not to extend the present note, we may shortly refer to our author's having already mentioned his grandfather (CALIGULA, c. xix.); besides other sources from which he drew his information. He tells us that he himself was then a boy. We have now arrived at the times in which his father bore a part. Such incidental notices, dropped by historical writers, have a certain value in enabling us to form a judgment on the genuineness of their narratives as to battle, being at that time an angusticlavian tribune in the thirteenth legion. He used frequently to say, that Otho, before his advancement to the empire, had such an abhorrence of civil war, that once, upon hearing an account given at table of the death of Cassius and Brutus, he fell into a trembling, and that he never would have interfered with Galba, but that he was confident of succeeding in his enterprise without a war. Moreover, that he was then encouraged to despise life by the example of a common soldier, who bringing news of the defeat of the army, and finding that he met with no credit, but was railed at for a liar and a coward, as if he had run away from the field of battle, fell upon his sword at the emperor's feet; upon the sight of which, my father said that Otho cried out, "that he would expose to no farther danger such brave men, who had deserved so well at his

---

contemporaneous, or recent, events.

hands." Advising therefore his brother, his brother's son, and the rest of his friends, to provide for their security in the best manner they could, after he had embraced and kissed them, he sent them away; and then withdrawing into a private room by himself, he wrote a letter of consolation to his sister, containing two sheets. He likewise sent another to Messalina, Nero's widow, whom he had intended to marry, committing to her the care of his relics and memory. He then burnt all the letters which he had by him, to prevent the danger and mischief that might otherwise befall the writers from the conqueror. What ready money he had, he distributed among his domestics.

XI. And now being prepared, and just upon the point of dispatching himself, he was induced to suspend the execution of his purpose by a great tumult which had broken out in the camp. Finding that some of the soldiers who were making off had been seized and detained as deserters,

"Let us add," said he, "this night to our life." These were his very words.

He then gave orders that no violence should be offered to any one; and keeping his chamber-door open until late at night, he allowed all who pleased the liberty to come and see him. At last, after quenching his thirst with a draught of cold water, he took up two poniards, and having examined the points of both, put one of them under his pillow, and shutting his chamber-door, slept very soundly, until, awaking about break of day, he stabbed himself under the left pap. Some persons bursting into the room upon his first groan, he at one time covered, and at another exposed his wound to the view of the bystanders, and thus life soon ebbed away. His funeral was hastily performed, according to his own order, in the thirty-eighth year of his age, and ninety-fifth day of his reign.[48]

---

48   A.U.C. 823.

XII. The person and appearance of Otho no way corresponded to the great spirit he displayed on this occasion; for he is said to have been of low stature, splay-footed, and bandy-legged. He was, however, effeminately nice in the care of his person: the hair on his body he plucked out by the roots; and because he was somewhat bald, he wore a kind of peruke, so exactly fitted to his head, that nobody could have known it for such. He used to shave every day, and rub his face with soaked bread; the use of which he began when the down first appeared upon his chin, to prevent his having any beard. It is said likewise that he celebrated publicly the sacred rites of Isis[49], clad in a linen garment, such as is

49   Jupiter, to prevent the discovery of his amour with Io, the daughter of the river Inachus, transformed her into a heifer, in which metamorphosis she was placed by Juno under the watchful inspection of Argus; but flying into Egypt, and her keeper being killed by Mercury,

used by the worshippers of that goddess. These circumstances, I imagine, caused the world to wonder the more that his death was so little in character with his life. Many of the soldiers who were present, kissing and bedewing with their tears his hands and feet as he lay dead, and celebrating him as "a most gallant man, and an incomparable emperor," immediately put an end to their own lives upon the spot, not far from his funeral pile.

Many of those likewise who were at a distance, upon hearing the news of his death, in the anguish of their hearts, began fighting amongst themselves, until they dispatched one another. To conclude: the

---

she recovered her human shape, and was married to Osiris. Her husband afterwards became a god of the Egyptians, and she a goddess, under the name of Isis. She was represented with a mural crown on her head, a cornucopia in one hand, and a sistrum (a musical instrument) in the other.

generality of mankind, though they hated him whilst living, yet highly extolled him after his death; insomuch that it was the common talk and opinion, "that Galba had been driven to destruction by his rival, not so much for the sake of reigning himself, as of restoring Rome to its ancient liberty."

*　*　*　*　*　*

It is remarkable, in the fortune of this emperor, that he owed both his elevation and catastrophe to the inextricable embarrassments in which he was involved; first, in respect of pecuniary circumstances, and next, of political. He was not, so far as we can learn, a follower of any of the sects of philosophers which justified, and even recommended suicide, in particular cases: yet he perpetrated that act with extraordinary coolness and resolution; and, what is no less remarkable, from the motive, as he avowed, of public expediency only. It was observed of him, for many years after his death, that "none ever died like Otho."

NINE

Aulus Vitellius

I. VERY DIFFERENT ACCOUNTS ARE given of the origin of the Vitellian family. Some describe it as ancient and noble, others as recent and obscure, nay, extremely mean. I am inclined to think, that these several representations have been made by the flatterers and detractors of Vitellius, after he became emperor, unless the fortunes of the family varied before.

There is extant a memoir addressed by Quintus Eulogius to Quintus Vitellius, quaestor to the Divine Augustus, in which it is said, that the Vitellii were descended from Faunus, king of the aborigines, and Vitellia[50], who was worshipped in many places as a goddess, and that they reigned formerly over the whole of Latium: that all who were left of the family removed out of the country of the Sabines to Rome, and were enrolled among the patricians: that

---

50   Faunus was supposed to be the third king who reigned over the original inhabitants of the central parts of Italy, Saturn being the first. Virgil makes his wife's name Marica—

Hunc Fauna, et nympha genitum
Laurente Marica Accipimus.–Aen. vii. 47.

Her name may have been changed after her deification; but we have no other accounts than those preserved by Suetonius, of several of the traditions handed down from the fabulous ages respecting the Vitellian family.

some monuments of the family continued a long time; as the Vitellian Way, reaching from the Janiculum to the sea, and likewise a colony of that name, which, at a very remote period of time, they desired leave from the government to defend against the Aequicolae[51], with a force raised by their own family only: also that, in the time of the war with the Samnites, some of the Vitellii who went with the troops levied for the security of Apulia, settled at Nuceria[52], and their descendants, a long time afterwards, returned again to Rome, and were admitted into the patrician order. On the other hand, the generality of writers say that the founder of the family was a freedman. Cassius

---

51 The Aequicolae were probably a tribe inhabiting the heights in the neighbourhood of Rome. Virgil describes them, Aen. vii. 746.

52 Nuceria, now Nocera, is a town near Mantua; but Livy, in treating of the war with the Samnites, always speaks of Luceria, which Strabo calls a town in Apulia.

Severus[53] and some others relate that he was likewise a cobbler, whose son having made a considerable fortune by agencies and dealings in confiscated property, begot, by a common strumpet, daughter of one Antiochus, a baker, a child, who afterwards became a Roman knight. Of these different accounts the reader is left to take his choice.

II. It is certain, however, that Publius Vitellius, of Nuceria, whether of an ancient family, or of low extraction, was a Roman knight, and a procurator to Augustus. He left behind him four sons, all men of very high station, who had the same cognomen, but the different praenomina of Aulus, Quintus, Publius, and Lucius. Aulus died in the enjoyment of the consulship[54], which office he bore jointly with Domitius, the father of Nero Caesar. He was elegant to excess in his manner of living, and notorious for the

---

53   Cassius Severus is mentioned before, in AUGUSTUS, c. lvi.; CALIGULA, c. xvi., etc.
54   A.U.C. 785.

vast expense of his entertainments. Quintus was deprived of his rank of senator, when, upon a motion made by Tiberius, a resolution passed to purge the senate of those who were in any respect not duly qualified for that honour. Publius, an intimate friend and companion of Germanicus, prosecuted his enemy and murderer, Cneius Piso, and procured sentence against him. After he had been made proctor, being arrested among the accomplices of Sejanus, and delivered into the hands of his brother to be confined in his house, he opened a vein with a penknife, intending to bleed himself to death. He suffered, however, the wound to be bound up and cured, not so much from repenting the resolution he had formed, as to comply with the importunity of his relations. He died afterwards a natural death during his confinement. Lucius, after his consulship[55], was made governor of Syria[56],

---

55   A.U.C. 787.

56   He is frequently commended by

and by his politic management not only brought Artabanus, king of the Parthians, to give him an interview, but to worship the standards of the Roman legions. He afterwards filled two ordinary consulships[57], and also the censorship[58] jointly with the emperor Claudius. Whilst that prince was absent upon his expedition into Britain[59], the care of the empire was committed to him, being a man of great integrity and industry. But he lessened his character not a little, by his passionate fondness for an abandoned freedwoman, with whose spittle, mixed with honey, he used to anoint his throat and jaws, by way of remedy for some complaint, not privately nor seldom, but daily and publicly. Being extravagantly prone to flattery, it was he who gave rise to the worship of Caius

---

Josephus for his kindness to the Jews. See, particularly, Antiq. VI. xviii.

57   A.U.C. 796, 800.

58   A.U.C. 801.

59   A.U.C. 797. See CLAUDIUS, c. xvii.

Caesar as a god, when, upon his return from Syria, he would not presume to accost him any otherwise than with his head covered, turning himself round, and then prostrating himself upon the earth. And to leave no artifice untried to secure the favour of Claudius, who was entirely governed by his wives and freedmen, he requested as the greatest favour from Messalina, that she would be pleased to let him take off her shoes; which, when he had done, he took her right shoe, and wore it constantly betwixt his toga and his tunic, and from time to time covered it with kisses. He likewise worshipped golden images of Narcissus and Pallas among his household gods. It was he, too, who, when Claudius exhibited the secular games, in his compliments to him upon that occasion, used this expression, "May you often do the same."

III. He died of palsy, the day after his seizure with it, leaving behind him two sons, whom he had by a most excellent and respectable wife, Sextilia. He had lived to see them both consuls, the same year and during the whole year also; the younger succeeding the elder for the last six months[60] The senate honoured him after his decease with a funeral at the public expense, and with a statue in the Rostra, which had this inscription upon the base: "One who was steadfast in his loyalty to his prince." The emperor Aulus Vitellius, the son of this Lucius, was born upon the eighth of the calends of October [24th September], or, as some say, upon the seventh of the ides of September [7th September], in the consulship of Drusus Caesar and Norbanus Flaccus[61]. His parents were so   terrified with the predictions of astrologers upon

---

60   A.U.C. 801.

61   A.U.C. 767; being the year after the death of the emperor Augustus; from whence it appears that Vitellius was seventeen years older than Otho, both being at an advanced age when they were raised to the imperial dignity.

the calculation of his nativity, that his father used his utmost endeavours to prevent his being sent governor into any of the provinces, whilst he was alive. His mother, upon his being sent to the legions[62], and also upon his being proclaimed emperor, immediately lamented him as utterly ruined. He spent his youth amongst the catamites of Tiberius at Capri, was himself constantly stigmatized with the name of Spintria[63], and was supposed to have been the occasion of his father's advancement, by consenting to gratify the emperor's unnatural lust.

IV. In the subsequent part of his life, being still most scandalously vicious, he rose to great favour at court; being upon a very intimate footing with Caius [Caligula], because of his fondness for chariot-driving, and with Claudius for his love of gaming. But he was in a still higher degree acceptable to Nero, as well on the same accounts, as

---

62   He was sent to Germany by Galba.
63   See TIBERIUS, c. xliii.

for a particular service which he rendered him. When Nero presided in the games instituted by himself, though he was extremely desirous to perform amongst the harpers, yet his modesty would not permit him, notwithstanding the people entreated much for it. Upon his quitting the theatre, Vitellius fetched him back again, pretending to represent the determined wishes of the people, and so afforded him the opportunity of yielding to their in treaties.

V. By the favour of these three princes, he was not only advanced to the great offices of state, but to the highest dignities of the sacred order; after which he held the proconsulship of Africa, and had the superintendence of the public works, in which appointment his conduct, and, consequently, his reputation, were very different. For he governed the province with singular integrity during two years, in the latter of which he acted as deputy to his brother, who succeeded him. But in his office in the city, he was said to pillage the temples of their gifts and ornaments, and to have exchanged brass and tin for gold and silver.[64]

VI. He took to wife Petronia, the daughter of a man of consular rank, and had by her a son named Petronius, who was blind of an eye. The mother being willing to appoint this youth her heir, upon condition that he should be released from his father's authority, the latter discharged him accordingly; but shortly after, as was believed, murdered him, charging him with a design upon his life, and pretending that he had, from consciousness of his guilt, drank the poison he had prepared for his father. Soon afterwards, he married Galeria Fundana, the daughter of a man of

---

64   Julius Caesar, also, was said to have exchanged brass for gold in the Capitol, Junius, c. liv. The tin which we here find in use at Rome, was probably brought from the Cassiterides, now the Scilly islands. whence it had been an article of commerce by the Phoenicians and Carthaginians from a very early period.

pretorian rank, and had by her both sons and daughters. Among the former was one who had such a stammering in his speech, that he was little better than if he had been dumb.

VII. He was sent by Galba into Lower Germany[65], contrary to his expectation. It is supposed that he was assisted in procuring this appointment by the interest of Titus Junius, a man of great influence at that time; whose friendship he had long before gained by favouring the same set of charioteers with him in the Circensian games. But Galba openly declared that none were less to be feared than those who only cared for their bellies, and that even his enormous appetite must be satisfied with the plenty of that province; so that it is evident he was selected for that government more out of contempt than kindness. It is certain, that when he was to set out, he had not

---

65   A.U.C. 821.

money for the expenses of his journey; he being at that time so much straitened in his circumstances, that he was obliged to put his wife and children, whom he left at Rome, into a poor lodging which he hired for them, in order that he might let his own house for the remainder of the year; and he pawned a pearl taken from his mother's ear-ring, to defray his expenses on the road. A crowd of creditors who were waiting to stop him, and amongst them the people of Sineussa and Formia, whose taxes he had converted to his own use, he eluded, by alarming them with the apprehension of false accusation. He had, however, sued a certain freedman, who was clamorous in demanding a debt of him, under pretence that he had kicked him; which action he would not withdraw, until he had wrung from the freedman fifty thousand sesterces. Upon his arrival in the province, the army, which was disaffected to Galba, and ripe for insurrection, received him with open arms, as if he had been sent them from heaven. It was no small recommendation to their favour, that he was the son of a man who had been thrice consul, was in the prime of life, and of an easy, prodigal disposition. This opinion, which had been long entertained of him, Vitellius confirmed by some late practices; having kissed all the common soldiers whom he met with upon the road, and been excessively complaisant in the inns and stables to the muleteers and travellers; asking them in a morning, if they had got their breakfasts, and letting them see, by belching, that he had eaten his.

VIII. After he had reached the camp, he denied no man any thing he asked for, and pardoned all who lay under sentence for disgraceful conduct or disorderly habits. Before a month, therefore, had passed, without regard to the day or season, he was hurried by the soldiers out of his bed-chamber, although it was evening, and he in an undress, and unanimously saluted by the title of EMPEROR[66]. He was then carried round the most considerable towns in the neighbourhood, with the sword of the Divine Julius in his hand; which had been taken by some person out of the temple of Mars, and presented to him when he was first saluted. Nor did he return to the pretorium, until his dining-room was in flames from the chimney's taking fire. Upon this accident, all being in consternation, and considering it as an unlucky omen, he cried out, "Courage, boys! it shines brightly upon us." And this was all he said to the soldiers. The army of the Upper Province likewise, which had before declared against Galba for the senate, joining in the proceedings, he very eagerly accepted the cognomen of Germanicus, offered him by the unanimous consent of both armies, but deferred assuming that of Augustus, and refused for ever that of Caesar.

IX. Intelligence of Galba's death arriving

---

66   A.U.C. 822.

soon after, when he had settled his affairs in Germany he divided his troops into two bodies, intending to send one of them before him against Otho, and to follow with the other himself. The army he sent forward had a lucky omen; for, suddenly, an eagle cams flying up to them on the right, and having hovered round the standards, flew gently before them on their road. But, on the other hand, when he began his own march, all the equestrian statues, which were erected for him in several places, fell suddenly down with their legs broken; and the laurel crown, which he had put on as emblematical of auspicious fortune, fell off his head into a river. Soon afterwards, at Vienne[67], as he was upon the tribunal administering justice, a cock perched upon his shoulder, and afterwards upon his head. The issue corresponded to these omens; for he was not able to keep

---

67   Vienne was a very ancient city of the province of Narbonne, famous in ecclesiastical history as the early seat of a bishopric in Gaul.

the empire which had been secured for him by his lieutenants.

X. He heard of the victory at Bedriacum[68], and the death of Otho, whilst he was yet in Gaul, and without the least hesitation, by a single proclamation, disbanded all the pretorian cohorts, as having, by their repeated treasons, set a dangerous example to the rest of the army; commanding them to deliver up their arms to his tribunes. A hundred and twenty of them, under whose hands he had found petitions presented to Otho, for rewards of their service in the murder of Galba, he besides ordered to be sought out and punished. So far his conduct deserved approbation, and was such as to afford hope of his becoming an excellent prince, had he not managed his other affairs in a way more corresponding with his own disposition, and his former manner of life, than to the imperial dignity. For, having begun his march, he rode

68   See OTHO, c. ix.

through every city in his route in a triumphal procession; and sailed down the rivers in ships, fitted out with the greatest elegance, and decorated with various kinds of crowns, amidst the most extravagant entertainments. Such was the want of discipline, and the licentiousness both in his family and army, that, not satisfied with the provision every where made for them at the public expense, they committed every kind of robbery and insult upon the inhabitants, setting slaves at liberty as they pleased; and if any dared to make resistance, they dealt blows and abuse, frequently wounds, and sometimes slaughter amongst them. When he reached the plains on which the battles were fought[69], some of those around him being offended at the smell of the carcases which lay rotting upon the ground, he had the audacity to encourage them by a most detestable remark, "That a dead enemy smelt not amiss, especially if he

---

69   See OTHO, c. ix.

were a fellow-citizen." To qualify, however, the offensiveness of the stench, he quaffed in public a goblet of wine, and with equal vanity and insolence distributed a large quantity of it among his troops. On his observing a stone with an inscription upon it to the memory of Otho, he said, "It was a mausoleum good enough for such a prince." He also sent the poniard, with which Otho killed himself, to the colony of Agrippina[70], to be dedicated to Mars. Upon the Appenine hills he celebrated a Bacchanalian feast.

XI. At last he entered the City with trumpets sounding, in his general's cloak, and girded with his sword, amidst a display of standards and banners; his attendants being all in the military habit, and the arms of the soldiers unsheathed. Acting more

---

70 Agrippina, the wife of Nero and mother of Germanicus, founded a colony on the Rhine at the place of her birth. Tacit. Annal. b. xii. It became a flourishing city, and its origin may be traced in its modern name, Cologne.

and more in open violation of all laws, both divine and human, he assumed the office of Pontifex Maximus, upon the day of the defeat at the Allia[71]; ordered the magistrates to be elected for ten years of office; and made himself consul for life. To put it out of all doubt what model he intended to follow in his government of the empire, he made his offerings to the shade of Nero in the midst of the Campus Martius, and with a full assembly of the public priests attending him. And at a solemn entertainment, he desired a harper who pleased the company much, to sing something in praise of Domitius; and upon his beginning some songs of Nero's, he started up in presence of the whole assembly, and could not refrain from

---

71   A dies non fastus, an unlucky day in the Roman calendar, being the anniversary of their great defeat by the Gauls on the river Allia, which joins the Tiber about five miles from Rome. This disaster happened on the 16th of the calends of August (17th July).

applauding him, by clapping his hands.

XII. After such a commencement of his career, he conducted his affairs, during the greater part of his reign, entirely by the advice and direction of the vilest amongst the players and charioteers, and especially his freedman Asiaticus. This fellow had, when young, been engaged with him in a course of mutual and unnatural pollution, but, being at last quite tired of the occupation, ran away. His master, some time after, caught him at Puteoli, selling a liquor called Posca[72], and put him in chains, but soon released him, and retained him in his former capacity. Growing weary, however, of his rough and stubborn temper, he sold him to a strolling fencing-master; after which, when the fellow was to have been brought up to play his part at the conclusion of an entertainment

---

72   Posca was sour wine or vinegar mixed with water, which was used by the Roman soldiery as their common drink. It has been found beneficial in the cure of putrid diseases.

of gladiators, he suddenly carried him off, and at length, upon his being advanced to the government of a province, gave him his freedom. The first day of his reign, he presented him with the gold rings at supper, though in the morning, when all about him requested that favour in his behalf, he expressed the utmost abhorrence of putting so great a stain upon the equestrian order.

XIII. He was chiefly addicted to the vices of luxury and cruelty. He always made three meals a day, sometimes four: breakfast, dinner, and supper, and a drunken revel after all. This load of victuals he could well enough bear, from a custom to which he had enured himself, of frequently vomiting. For these several meals he would make different appointments at the houses of his friends on the same day. None ever entertained him at less expense than four hundred thousand sesterces[73]. The most famous was a set

---

73   Upwards of 4000 pounds sterling. See note, p. 487.

entertainment given him by his brother, at which, it is said, there were served up no less than two thousand choice fishes, and seven thousand birds. Yet even this supper he himself outdid, at a feast which he gave upon the first use of a dish which had been made for him, and which, for its extraordinary size, he called "The Shield of Minerva." In this dish there were tossed up together the livers of char-fish, the brains of pheasants and peacocks, with the tongues of flamingos, and the entrails of lampreys, which had been brought in ships of war as far as from the Carpathian Sea, and the Spanish Straits. He was not only a man of an insatiable appetite, but would gratify it likewise at unseasonable times, and with any garbage that came in his way; so that, at a sacrifice, he would snatch from the fire flesh and cakes, and eat them upon the spot. When he travelled, he did the same at the inns upon the road, whether the meat was fresh dressed and hot, or what had been left the day before, and was half-eaten.

XIV. He delighted in the infliction of punishments, and even those which were capital, without any distinction of persons or occasions. Several noblemen, his school-fellows and companions, invited by him to court, he treated with such flattering caresses, as seemed to indicate an affection short only of admitting them to share the honours of the imperial dignity; yet he put them all to death by some base means or other. To one he gave poison with his own hand, in a cup of cold water which he called for in a fever. He scarcely spared one of all the usurers, notaries, and publicans, who had ever demanded a debt of him at Rome, or any toll or custom upon the road. One of these, while in the very act of saluting him, he ordered for execution, but immediately sent for him back; upon which all about him applauding his clemency, he commanded him to be slain in his own presence, saying, "I have a mind to feed my eyes." Two sons who interceded for their father, he ordered to be executed with him. A Roman knight, upon his being dragged away for execution, and crying out to him, "You are my heir," he desired to produce his will: and finding that he had made his freedman joint heir with him, he commanded that both he and the freedman should have their throats cut. He put to death some of the common people for cursing aloud the blue party in the Circensian games; supposing it to be done in contempt of himself, and the expectation of a revolution in the government. There were no persons he was more severe against than jugglers and astrologers; and as soon as any one of them was informed against, he put him to death without the formality of a trial. He was enraged against them, because, after his proclamation by which he commanded all astrologers to quit home, and Italy also, before the calends [the first] of October, a bill was immediately posted about the city, with the following words:–"TAKE NOTICE:[74] The Chaldaeans also decree that Vitellius Germanicus shall be no more, by the day of the said calends." He was even suspected of being accessary to his mother's death, by forbidding sustenance to be given her when she was unwell; a German witch[75], whom he held to be oracular, having told him, "That he would long reign in security if he survived his mother." But others say, that being quite weary of the state of affairs, and apprehensive of the future, she obtained without difficulty a dose of poison from her son.

XV. In the eighth month of his reign,

---

74   In imitation of the form of the public edicts, which began with the words, BONUM FACTUM.

75   Catta muliere: The Catti were a German tribe who inhabited the present countries of Hesse or Baden. Tacitus, De Mor. Germ., informs us that the Germans placed great confidence in the prophetical inspirations which they attributed to their women.

the troops both in Moesia and Pannonia revolted from him; as did likewise, of the armies beyond sea, those in Judaea and Syria, some of which swore allegiance to Vespasian as emperor in his own presence, and others in his absence. In order, therefore, to secure the favour and affection of the people, Vitellius lavished on all around whatever he had it in his power to bestow, both publicly and privately, in the most extravagant manner. He also levied soldiers in the city, and promised all who enlisted as volunteers, not only their discharge after the victory was gained, but all the rewards due to veterans who had served their full time in the wars. The enemy now pressing forward both by sea and land, on one hand he opposed against them his brother with a fleet, the new levies, and a body of gladiators, and in another quarter the troops and generals who were engaged at Bedriacum. But being beaten or betrayed in every direction, he agreed with Flavius Sabinus, Vespasian's brother, to abdicate, on condition of having his life spared, and a hundred millions of sesterces granted him; and he immediately, upon the palace-steps, publicly declared to a large body of soldiers there assembled, "that he resigned the government, which he had accepted reluctantly;" but they all remonstrating against it, he deferred the conclusion of the treaty. Next day, early in the morning, he came down to the Forum in a very mean habit, and with many tears repeated the declaration from a writing which he held in his hand; but the soldiers and people again interposing, and encouraging him not to give way, but to rely on their zealous support, he recovered his courage, and forced Sabinus, with the rest of the Flavian party, who now thought themselves secure, to retreat into the Capitol, where he destroyed them all by setting fire to the temple of Jupiter, whilst he beheld the contest and the fire from

Tiberius's house[76], where he was feasting. Not long after, repenting of what he had done, and throwing the blame of it upon others, he called a meeting, and swore "that nothing was dearer to him than the public peace;" which oath he also obliged the rest to take. Then drawing a dagger from his side, he presented it first to the consul, and, upon his refusing it, to the magistrates, and then to every one of the senators; but none of them being willing to accept it, he went away, as if he meant to lay it up in the temple of Concord; but some crying out to him, "You are Concord," he

---

76   Suetonius does not supply any account of the part added by Tiberius to the palace of the Caesars on the Palatine, although, as it will be recollected, he has mentioned or described the works of Augustus, Caligula, and Nero. The banquetting-room here mentioned would easily command a view of the Capitol, across the narrow intervening valley. Flavius Sabinus, Vespasian's brother, was prefect of the city.

came back again, and said that he would not only keep his weapon, but for the future use the cognomen of Concord.

XVI. He advised the senate to send deputies, accompanied by the Vestal Virgins, to desire peace, or, at least, time for consultation. The day after, while he was waiting for an answer, he received intelligence by a scout, that the enemy was advancing. Immediately, therefore, throwing himself into a small litter, borne by hand, with only two attendants, a baker and a cook, he privately withdrew to his father's house, on the Aventine hill, intending to escape thence into Campania. But a groundless report being circulated, that the enemy was willing to come to terms, he suffered himself to be carried back to the palace. Finding, however, nobody there, and those who were with him stealing away, he girded round his waist a belt full of gold pieces, and then ran into the porter's lodge, tying the dog before the door, and piling up against it the bed and bedding.

XVII. By this time the forerunners of the enemy's army had broken into the palace, and meeting with nobody, searched, as was natural, every corner. Being dragged by them out of his cell, and asked "who he was?" (for they did not recognize him), "and if he knew where Vitellius was?" he deceived them by a falsehood. But at last being discovered, he begged hard to be detained in custody, even were it in a prison; pretending to have something to say which concerned Vespasian's security. Nevertheless, he was dragged half-naked into the Forum, with his hands tied behind him, a rope about his neck, and his clothes torn, amidst the most contemptuous abuse, both by word and deed, along the Via Sacra; his head being held back by the hair, in the manner of condemned criminals, and the point of a sword put under his chin, that he might hold up his face to public view;

some of the mob, meanwhile, pelting him with dung and mud, whilst others called him "an incendiary and glutton." They also upbraided him with the defects of his person, for he was monstrously tall, and had a face usually very red with hard-drinking, a large belly, and one thigh weak, occasioned by a chariot running against him, as he was attending upon Caius[77], while he was driving. At length, upon the Scalae Gemoniae, he was tormented and put to death in lingering tortures, and then dragged by a hook into the Tiber.

XVIII. He perished with his brother and son[78], in the fifty-seventh year of his age[79], and verified the prediction of those who, from the omen which happened to him at

---

77   Caligula.

78   Lucius and Germanicus, the brother and son of Vitellius, were slain near Terracina; the former was marching to his brother's relief.

79   A.U.C. 822.

Vienne, as before related[80], foretold that he would be made prisoner by some man of Gaul. For he was seized by Antoninus Primus, a general of the adverse party, who was born at Toulouse, and, when a boy, had the cognomen of Becco[81], which signifies a cock's beak.

*   *   *   *   *   *

After the extinction of the race of the Caesars, the possession of the imperial power became extremely precarious; and great influence in the army was the means which now invariably led to the throne. The

---

80   c. ix.

81   Becco, from whence the French bec, and English beak; with, probably, the family names of Bec or Bek. This distinguished provincial, under his Latin name of Antoninus Primus, commanded the seventh legion in Gaul. His character is well drawn by Tacitus, in his usual terse style, Hist. XI. 86. 2.

soldiers having arrogated to themselves the right of nomination, they either unanimously elected one and the same person, or different parties supporting the interests of their respective favourites, there arose between them a contention, which was usually determined by an appeal to arms, and followed by the assassination of the unsuccessful competitor. Vitellius, by being a parasite of all the emperors from Tiberius to Nero inclusively, had risen to a high military rank, by which, with a spirit of enterprise, and large promises to the soldiery, it was not difficult to snatch the reins of government, while they were yet fluctuating in the hands of Otho. His ambition prompted to the attempt, and his boldness was crowned with success. In the service of the four preceding emperors, Vitellius had imbibed the principal vices of them all: but what chiefly distinguished him was extreme voraciousness, which, though he usually pampered it with enormous luxury, could yet be gratified by the vilest and most offensive garbage. The pusillanimity discovered by this emperor at his death, forms a striking contrast to the heroic behaviour of Otho.

TEN

T. Flavius Vespasianus
Augustus

I. THE EMPIRE, WHICH HAD been long thrown into a disturbed and unsetted state, by the rebellion and violent death of its three last rulers, was at length restored to peace and security by the Flavian family, whose descent was indeed obscure, and which boasted no ancestral honours;

but the public had no cause to regret its elevation; though it is acknowledged that Domitian met with the just reward of his avarice and cruelty. Titus Flavius Petro, a townsman of Reate[82], whether a centurion or an evocatus[83] of Pompey's party in the civil war, is uncertain, fled out of the battle of Pharsalia and went home; where, having at last obtained his pardon and discharge, he became a collector of the money raised by public sales in the way of auction. His son, surnamed Sabinus, was never engaged in the military service, though some say

------

82   Reate, the original seat of the Flavian family, was a city of the Sabines. Its present name is Rieti.

83   It does not very clearly appear what rank in the Roman armies was held by the evocati. They are mentioned on three occasions by Suetonius, without affording us much assistance. Caesar, like our author, joins them with the centurions. See, in particular, De Bell. Civil. I. xvii. 4.

he was a centurion of the first order, and others, that whilst he held that rank, he was discharged on account of his bad state of health: this Sabinus, I say, was a publican, and received the tax of the fortieth penny in Asia. And there were remaining, at the time of the advancement of the family, several statues, which had been erected to him by the cities of that province, with this inscription: "To the honest Tax-farmer."[84] He afterwards turned usurer amongst the Helvetii, and there died, leaving behind him his wife, Vespasia Pella, and two sons by her; the elder of whom, Sabinus, came to be prefect of the city, and the younger, Vespasian, to be emperor. Polla, descended of a good family, at Nursia[85], had for her father Vespasius Pollio, thrice

---

84   The inscription was in Greek, kalos telothaesanti.

85   In the ancient Umbria, afterwards the duchy of Spoleto; its modern name being Norcia.

appointed   military tribune, and at last prefect of the camp; and her brother was a senator of praetorian dignity. There is to this day, about six miles from Nursia, on the road to Spoletum, a place on the summit of a hill, called Vespasiae, where are several monuments of the Vespasii, a sufficient proof of the splendour and antiquity of the family. I will not deny that some have pretended to say, that Petro's father was a native of Gallia Transpadana[86], whose employment was to hire workpeople who used to emigrate every year from the country of the Umbria into that of the Sabines, to assist them in their husbandry[87]; but who settled at last in

---

86   Gaul beyond, north of the Po, now Lombardy.

87   We find the annual migration of labourers in husbandry a very common practice in ancient as well as in modern times. At present, several thousand industrious labourers cross over every summer from the duchies of Parma and Modena, bordering on the district mentioned by

the town of Reate, and there married. But of this I have not been able to discover the least proof, upon the strictest inquiry.

II. Vespasian was born in the country of the Sabines, beyond Reate, in a little country-seat called Phalacrine, upon the fifth of the calends of December [27th November], in the evening, in the consulship of Quintus Sulpicius Camerinus and Caius Poppaeus Sabinus, five years before the death of Augustus[88]; and was educated under the care of Tertulla, his grandmother by the father's side, upon an estate belonging to the family, at Cosa[89]. After his advancement to the empire, he used frequently to visit the place where he had spent his infancy;

Suetonius, to the island of Corsica; returning to the continent when the harvest is got in.

88   A.U.C. 762, A.D. 10.

89   Cosa was a place in the Volscian territory; of which Anagni was probably the chief town. It lies about forty miles to the north-east of Rome.

and the villa was continued in the same condition, that he might see every thing about him just as he had been used to do. And he had so great a regard for the memory of his grandmother, that, upon solemn occasions and festival days, he constantly drank out of a silver cup which she had been accustomed to use. After assuming the manly habit, he had a long time a distaste for the senatorian toga, though his brother had obtained it; nor could he be persuaded by any one but his mother to sue for that badge of honour. She at length drove him to it, more by taunts and reproaches, than by her entreaties and authority, calling him now and then, by way of reproach, his brother's footman. He served as military tribune in Thrace. When made quaestor, the province of Crete and Cyrene fell to him by lot. He was candidate for the aedileship, and soon after for the praetorship, but met with a repulse in the former case; though at last, with much difficulty, he came in sixth on the poll-books. But the office of praetor he carried upon his first canvass, standing amongst the highest at the poll. Being incensed against the senate, and desirous to gain, by all possible means, the good graces of Caius[90], he obtained leave to exhibit extraordinary[91] games for the emperor's victory in Germany, and advised them to increase the punishment of the conspirators against his life, by exposing their corpses unburied. He likewise gave him thanks in that august assembly for the honour of being admitted to his table.

III. Meanwhile, he married Flavia Domitilla, who had formerly been the mistress of Statilius Capella, a Roman knight of Sabrata in Africa, who [Domitilla] enjoyed Latin rights; and was soon after declared fully and freely a citizen of Rome, on a

---

90   Caligula.

91   These games were extraordinary, as being out of the usual course of those given by praetors.

trial before the court of Recovery, brought by her father Flavius Liberalis, a native of Ferentum, but no more than secretary to a quaestor. By her he had the following children: Titus, Domitian, and Domitilla. He outlived his wife and daughter, and lost them both before he became emperor. After the death of his wife, he renewed his union[92] with his former concubine Caenis,

---

92   "Revocavit in contubernium." From the difference of our habits, there is no word in the English language which exactly conveys the meaning of contubernium; a word which, in a military sense, the Romans applied to the intimate fellowship between comrades in war who messed together, and lived in close fellowship in the same tent. Thence they transferred it to a union with one woman who was in a higher position than a concubine, but, for some reason, could not acquire the legal rights of a wife, as in the case of slaves of either sex. A man of rank, also, could not marry a slave or a freedwoman, however much he might be attached to her.

the freedwoman of Antonia, and also her amanuensis, and treated her, even after he was emperor, almost as if she had been his lawful wife.[93]

IV. In the reign of Claudius, by the interest of Narcissus, he was sent to Germany, in command of a legion; whence being removed into Britain, he engaged the enemy in thirty several battles. He reduced under subjection to the Romans two very powerful tribes, and above twenty great towns, with the Isle of Wight, which lies close to the coast of Britain; partly under the command of Aulus Plautius, the consular lieutenant, and partly under

---

93   Nearly the same phrases are applied by Suetonius to Drusilla, see CALIGULA, c. xxiv., and to Marcella, the concubine of Commodus, by Herodian, I. xvi. 9., where he says that she had all the honours of an empress, except that the incense was not offered to her. These connections resembled the left-hand marriages of the German princes.

Claudius himself[94]. For this success he received the triumphal ornaments, and in a short time after two priesthoods, besides the consulship, which he held during the two last months of the year[95]. The interval between that and his proconsulship he spent in leisure and retirement, for fear of Agrippina, who still held great sway over her son, and hated all the friends of Narcissus, who was then dead. Afterwards

94   This expedition to Britain has been mentioned before, CLAUDIUS, c. xvii. and note; and see ib. xxiv.] Valerius Flaccus, i. 8, and Silius Italicus, iii. 598, celebrate the triumphs of Vespasian in Britain. In representing him, however, as carrying his arms among the Caledonian tribes, their flattery transferred to the emperor the glory of the victories gained by his lieutenant, Agricola. Vespasian's own conquests, while he served in Britain, were principally in the territories of the Brigantes, lying north of the Humber, and including the present counties of York and Durham.
95   A.U.C. 804.

he got by lot the province of Africa, which he governed with great reputation, excepting that once, in an insurrection at Adrumetum, he was pelted with turnips. It is certain that he returned thence nothing richer; for his credit was so low, that he was obliged to mortgage his whole property to his brother, and was reduced to the necessity of dealing in mules, for the support of his rank; for which reason he was commonly called "the Muleteer." He is said likewise to have been convicted of extorting from a young man of fashion two hundred thousand sesterces for procuring him the broad-stripe, contrary to the wishes of his father, and was severely reprimanded for it. While in attendance upon Nero in Achaia, he frequently withdrew from the theatre while Nero was singing, and went to sleep if he remained, which gave so much offence, that he was not only excluded from his society, but debarred the liberty of saluting him in public. Upon this, he retired to a small out-of-the-way town, where he lay skulking in constant fear of his life, until a province, with an army, was offered him.

A firm persuasion had long prevailed through all the East[96], that it was fated

---

96   Tacitus, Hist. V. xiii. 3., mentions this ancient prediction, and its currency through the East, in nearly the same terms as Suetonius. The coming power is in both instances described in the plural number, profecti; "those shall come forth;" and Tacitus applies it to Titus as well as Vespasian. The prophecy is commonly supposed to have reference to a passage in Micah, v. 2, "Out of thee (Bethlehem-Ephrata) shall He come forth, to be ruler in Israel." Earlier prophetic intimations of a similar character, and pointing to a more extended dominion, have been traced in the sacred records of the Jews; and there is reason to believe that these books were at this time not unknown in the heathen world, particularly at Alexandria, and through the Septuagint version. These predictions, in their literal sense, point to the establishment of a universal monarchy, which should take its rise in Judaea. The Jews looked for their

for the empire of the world, at that time, to devolve on some who should go forth from Judaea. This prediction referred to a Roman emperor, as the event shewed; but the Jews, applying it to themselves, broke out into rebellion, and having defeated and slain their governor[97], routed the lieutenant

---

accomplishment in the person of one of their own nation, the expected Messiah, to which character there were many pretenders in those times. The first disciples of Christ, during the whole period of his ministry, supposed that they were to be fulfilled in him. The Romans thought that the conditions were answered by Vespasian, and Titus having been called from Judaea to the seat of empire. The expectations entertained by the Jews, and naturally participated in and appropriated by the first converts to Christianity, having proved groundless, the prophecies were subsequently interpreted in a spiritual sense.

97   Gessius Florus was at that time governor of Judaea, with the title and rank of prepositus, it not being a proconsular province,

of Syria[98], a man of consular rank, who was advancing to his assistance, and took an eagle, the standard, of one of his legions. As the suppression of this revolt appeared to require a stronger force and an active general, who might be safely trusted in an affair of so much importance, Vespasian was chosen in preference to all others, both for his known activity, and on account of the obscurity of his origin and name, being a person of whom there could be not the least jealousy. Two legions, therefore, eight squadrons of horse, and ten cohorts, being added to the former troops in Judaea, and, taking with him his eldest son as lieutenant, as soon as he arrived in his province, he turned the eyes of the neighbouring provinces upon

---

as the native princes still held some parts of it, under the protection and with the alliance of the Romans. Gessius succeeded Florus Albinus, the successor of Felix.

98   Cestius Gallus was consular lieutenant in Syria.

him, by reforming immediately the discipline of the camp, and engaging the enemy once or twice with such resolution, that, in the attack of a castle[99], he had his knee hurt by the stroke of a stone, and received several arrows in his shield.

V. After the deaths of Nero and Galba, whilst Otho and Vitellius were contending for the sovereignty, he entertained hopes of obtaining the empire, with the prospect of which he had long before flattered himself, from the following omens. Upon an estate belonging to the Flavian family, in the neighbourhood of Rome, there was an old oak, sacred to Mars, which, at the three several deliveries of Vespasia, put out each time a new branch; evident intimations of the future fortune of each child. The first was but a slender one, which quickly withered away; and accordingly, the girl that was born did not live long. The second became vigorous,

---

99   See note to c. vii.

which portended great good fortune; but the third grew like a tree. His father, Sabinus, encouraged by these omens, which were confirmed by the augurs, told his mother, "that her grandson would be emperor of Rome;" at which she laughed heartily, wondering, she said, "that her son should be in his dotage whilst she continued still in full possession of her faculties."

Afterwards in his aedileship, when Caius Caesar, being enraged at his not taking care to have the streets kept clean, ordered the soldiers to fill the bosom of his gown with dirt, some persons at that time construed it into a sign that the government, being trampled under foot and deserted in some civil commotion, would fall under his protection, and as it were into his lap. Once, while he was at dinner, a strange dog, that wandered about the streets, brought a man's hand[100],

---

100   A right hand was the sign of sovereign power, and, as every one knows, borne upon a staff among the standards of the armies.

and laid it under the table. And another time, while he was at supper, a plough-ox throwing the yoke off his neck, broke into the room, and after he had frightened away all the attendants, on a sudden, as if he was tired, fell down at his feet, as he lay still upon his couch, and hung down his neck. A cypress-tree likewise, in a field belonging to the family, was torn up by the roots, and laid flat upon the ground, when there was no violent wind; but next day it rose again fresher and stronger than before.

He dreamt in Achaia that the good fortune of himself and his family would begin when Nero had a tooth drawn; and it happened that the day after, a surgeon coming into the hall, showed him a tooth which he had just extracted from Nero. In Judaea, upon his consulting the oracle of the divinity at Carmel[101], the answer was so encouraging

---

101   Tacitus says, "Carmel is the name both of a god and a mountain; but there is neither image nor temple of the god; such are the

as to assure him of success in anything he projected, however great or important it might be. And when Josephus[102], one of the noble prisoners, was put in chains, he confidently affirmed that he should be released in a very short time by the same Vespasian, but he would be emperor first[103]. Some omens were likewise mentioned in

---

ancient traditions; we find there only an altar and religious awe."–Hist. xi. 78, 4. It also appears, from his account, that Vespasian offered sacrifice on Mount Carmel, where Basilides, mentioned hereafter, c. vii., predicted his success from an inspection of the entrails.

102 Josephus, the celebrated Jewish historian, who was engaged in these wars, having been taken prisoner, was confined in the dungeon at Jotapata, the castle referred to in the preceding chapter, before which Vespasian was wounded.–De Bell. cxi. 14.

103 The prediction of Josephus was founded on the Jewish prophecies mentioned in the note to c. iv., which he, like others, applied to Vespasian.

the news from Rome, and among others, that Nero, towards the close of his days, was commanded in a dream to carry Jupiter's sacred chariot out of the sanctuary where it stood, to Vespasian's house, and conduct it thence into the circus. Also not long afterwards, as Galba was going to the election, in which he was created consul for the second time, a statue of the Divine Julius[104] turned towards the east. And in the field of Bedriacum[105], before the battle began, two eagles engaged in the sight of the army; and one of them being beaten, a third came from the east, and drove away the conqueror.

VI. He made, however, no attempt upon the sovereignty, though his friends were very ready to support him, and even pressed him

---

104   Julius Caesar is always called by our author after his apotheosis, Divus Julius.
105   The battle at Bedriacum secured the Empire for Vitellius. See OTHO, c. ix; VITELLIUS, c. x.

to the enterprise, until he was encouraged to it by the fortuitous aid of persons unknown to him and at a distance. Two thousand men, drawn out of three legions in the Moesian army, had been sent to the assistance of Otho. While they were upon their march, news came that he had been defeated, and had put an end to his life; notwithstanding which they continued their march as far as Aquileia, pretending that they gave no credit to the report. There, tempted by the opportunity which the disorder of the times afforded them, they ravaged and plundered the country at discretion; until at length, fearing to be called to an account on their return, and punished for it, they resolved upon choosing and creating an emperor. "For they were no ways inferior," they said, "to the army which made Galba emperor, nor to the pretorian troops which had set up Otho, nor the army in Germany, to whom Vitellius owed his elevation." The names of all the consular lieutenants, therefore, being taken into consideration, and one objecting to one, and another to another, for various reasons; at last some of the third legion, which a little before Nero's death had been removed out of Syria into Moesia, extolled Vespasian in high terms; and all the rest assenting, his name was immediately inscribed on their standards. The design was nevertheless quashed for a time, the troops being brought to submit to Vitellius a little longer.

However, the fact becoming known, Tiberius Alexander, governor of Egypt, first obliged the legions under his command to swear obedience to Vespasian as their emperor, on the calends [the 1st] of July, which was observed ever after as the day of his accession to the empire; and upon the fifth of the ides of the same month [the 28th July], the army in Judaea, where he then was, also swore allegiance to him. What contributed greatly to forward the affair, was a copy of a letter, whether real or counterfeit, which was circulated, and said to have been written by Otho before his decease to Vespasian, recommending to him in the most urgent terms to avenge his death, and entreating him to come to the aid of the commonwealth; as well as a report which was circulated, that Vitellius, after his success against Otho, proposed to change the winter quarters of the legions, and remove those in Germany to a less hazardous station and a warmer climate. Moreover, amongst the governors of provinces, Licinius Mucianus dropping the grudge arising from a jealousy of which he had hitherto made no secret, promised to join him with the Syrian army, and, among the allied kings, Volugesus, king of the Parthians, offered him a reinforcement of forty thousand archers.

VII. Having, therefore, entered on a civil war, and sent forward his generals and forces into Italy, he himself, in the meantime, passed over to Alexandria, to obtain possession of the key of Egypt[106]. Here having entered alone, without attendants, the temple of Serapis, to take the auspices respecting the establishment of his power, and having done his utmost to propitiate the deity, upon turning round, [his freedman] Basilides[107] appeared before him, and seemed to

---

106   Alexandria may well be called the key, claustra, of Egypt, which was the granary of Rome. It was of the first importance that Vespasian should secure it at this juncture.

107   Tacitus describes Basilides as a man of rank among the Egyptians, and he appears also to have been a priest, as we find him officiating at Mount Carmel, c. v. This is so incompatible with his being a Roman freedman, that commentators concur in supposing that the word "libertus." although found in all the copies now extant, has crept into the text by some inadvertence of an early transcriber. Basilides appears, like Philo Judaeus, who lived about the same period, to have been half-Greek, half-Jew, and to have belonged to the celebrated Platonic school of Alexandria.

offer him the sacred leaves, chaplets, and cakes, according to the usage of the place, although no one had admitted him, and he had long laboured under a muscular debility, which would hardly have allowed him to walk into the temple; besides which, it was certain that at the very time he was far away. Immediately after this, arrived letters with intelligence that Vitellius's troops had been defeated at Cremona, and he himself slain at Rome. Vespasian, the new emperor, having been raised unexpectedly from a low estate, wanted something which might clothe him with divine majesty and authority. This, likewise, was now added. A poor man who was blind, and another who was lame, came both together before him, when he was seated on the tribunal, imploring him to heal them[108], and saying that they were

---

108 Tacitus informs us that Vespasian himself believed Basilides to have been at this time not only in an infirm state of health, but at the distance of several days' journey from

admonished in a dream by the god Serapis to seek his aid, who assured them that he would restore sight to the one by anointing his eyes with his spittle, and give strength to the leg of the other, if he vouchsafed but to touch it with his heel. At first he could scarcely believe that the thing would any how succeed, and therefore hesitated to venture on making the experiment. At length, however, by the advice of his friends, he made the attempt publicly, in the presence of the assembled multitudes, and it was

---

Alexandria. But (for his greater satisfaction) he strictly examined the priests whether Basilides had entered the temple on that day: he made inquiries of all he met, whether he had been seen in the city; nay, further, he dispatched messengers on horseback, who ascertained that at the time specified, Basilides was more than eighty miles from Alexandria. Then Vespasian comprehended that the appearance of Basilides, and the answer to his prayers given through him, were by divine interposition. Tacit. Hist. iv. 82. 2.

T. Flavius Vespasianus Augustus

crowned with success in both cases[109].

---

109   The account given by Tacitus of the miracles of Vespasian is fuller than that of Suetonius, but does not materially vary in the details, except that, in his version of the story, he describes the impotent man to be lame in the hand, instead of the leg or the knee, and adds an important circumstance in the case of the blind man, that he was "notus tabe occulorum," notorious for the disease in his eyes. He also winds up the narrative with the following statement: "They who were present, relate both these cures, even at this time, when there is nothing to be gained by lying." Both the historians lived within a few years of the occurrence, but their works were not published until advanced periods of their lives. The closing remark of Tacitus seems to indicate that, at least, he did not entirely discredit the account; and as for Suetonius, his pages are as full of prodigies of all descriptions, related apparently in all good faith, as a monkish chronicle of the Middle Ages. The story has the more interest, as it is one of the examples of successful imposture, selected by Hume in his Essay on

Miracles; with the reply to which by Paley, in his Evidences of Christianity, most readers are familiar. The commentators on Suetonius agree with Paley in considering the whole affair as a juggle between the priests, the patients, and, probably, the emperor. But what will, perhaps, strike the reader as most remarkable, is the singular coincidence of the story with the accounts given of several of the miracles of Christ; whence it has been supposed, that the scene was planned in imitation of them. It did not fall within the scope of Dr. Paley's argument to advert to this; and our own brief illustration must be strictly confined within the limits of historical disquisition. Adhering to this principle, we may point out that if the idea of plagiarism be accepted, it receives some confirmation from the incident related by our author in a preceding paragraph, forming, it may be considered, another scene of the same drama, where we find Basilides appearing to Vespasian in the temple of Serapis, under circumstances which cannot fail to remind us of Christ's suddenly standing in the midst of his disciples, "when the doors were shut." This incident, also, has very much the appearance of a parody on the evangelical history. But if the striking similarity of the two narratives be thus accounted for, it is remarkable that while the priests of Alexandria, or, perhaps, Vespasian himself from his residence in Judaea, were in possession of such exact details of two of Christ's miracles–if not of a third striking incident in his history–we should find not the most distant allusion in the works of such cotemporary writers as Tacitus and Suetonius, to any one of the still more stupendous occurrences which had recently taken place in a part of the world with which the Romans had now very intimate relations. The character of these authors induces us to hesitate in adopting the notion, that either contempt or disbelief would have led them to pass over such events, as altogether unworthy of notice; and the only other inference from their silence is, that they had never heard of them. But as this can scarcely be reconciled with the plagiarism attributed to Vespasian or the Egyptian priests, it is safer to conclude that the coincidence, however singular, was merely fortuitous. It may be added that Spartianus, who wrote the lives of Adrian and succeeding emperors, gives an account of a similar miracle

About the same time, at Tegea in Arcadia, by the direction of some soothsayers, several vessels of ancient workmanship were dug out of a consecrated place, on which there was an effigy resembling Vespasian.

VIII. Returning now to Rome, under these auspices, and with a great reputation, after enjoying a triumph for victories over the Jews, he added eight consulships[110] to his former one. He likewise assumed the censorship, and made it his principal concern, during the whole of his government, first to restore order in the state, which had been almost ruined, and was in a tottering condition, and then to improve it. The soldiers, one part of them emboldened by victory, and the other smarting with the disgrace of their defeat, had abandoned themselves to every species of licentiousness and insolence. Nay, the provinces, too, and free cities,

---

performed by that prince in healing a blind man.
110   A.U.C. 823-833, excepting 826 and 831.

and some kingdoms in alliance with Rome, were all in a disturbed state. He, therefore, disbanded many of Vitellius's soldiers, and punished others; and so far was he from granting any extraordinary favours to the sharers of his success, that it was late before he paid the gratuities due to them by law. That he might let slip no opportunity of reforming the discipline of the army, upon a young man's coming much perfumed to return him thanks for having appointed him to command a squadron of horse, he turned away his head in disgust, and, giving him this sharp reprimand, "I had rather you had smelt of garlic," revoked his commission. When the men belonging to the fleet, who travelled by turns from Ostia and Puteoli to Rome, petitioned for an addition to their pay, under the name of shoe-money, thinking that it would answer little purpose to send them away without a reply, he ordered them for the future to run barefooted; and so they have done ever since. He deprived of their liberties, Achaia, Lycia, Rhodes, Byzantium, and Samos; and reduced them into the form of provinces; Thrace, also, and Cilicia, as well as Comagene, which until that time had been under the government of kings. He stationed some legions in Cappadocia on account of the frequent inroads of the barbarians, and, instead of a Roman knight, appointed as governor of it a man of consular rank. The ruins of houses which had been burnt down long before, being a great desight to the city, he gave leave to any one who would, to take possession of the void ground and build upon it, if the proprietors should hesitate to perform the work themselves. He resolved upon rebuilding the Capitol, and was the foremost to put his hand to clearing the ground of the rubbish, and removed some of it upon his own shoulder. And he undertook, likewise, to restore the three thousand tables of brass which had been destroyed in the fire which consumed the Capitol; searching in all quarters for copies of those curious and ancient records, in which were contained the decrees of the senate, almost from the building of the city, as well as the acts of the people, relative to alliances, treaties, and privileges granted to any person.

IX. He likewise erected several new public buildings, namely, the temple of Peace[111]

---

111   The temple of Peace, erected A.D. 71, on the conclusion of the wars with the Germans and the Jews, was the largest temple in Rome. Vespasian and Titus deposited in it the sacred vessels and other spoils which were carried in their triumph after the conquest of Jerusalem. They were consumed, and the temple much damaged, if not destroyed, by fire, towards the end of the reign of Commodus, in the year 191. It stood in the Forum, where some ruins on a prodigious scale, still remaining, were traditionally considered to be those of the Temple of Peace, until Piranesi contended that they are part of Nero's Golden House. Others suppose that they are the remains of a Basilica. A beautiful fluted Corinthian column,

near the Forum, that of Claudius on the Coelian mount, which had been begun by Agrippina, but almost entirely demolished by Nero[112]; and an amphitheatre[113] in the middle of the city, upon finding that Augustus had projected such a work. He purified the senatorian and equestrian orders, which

---

forty-seven feet high, which was removed from this spot, and now stands before the church of S. Maria Maggiore, gives a great idea of the splendour of the original structure.

112   This temple, converted into a Christian church by pope Simplicius, who flourished, A.D. 464-483, preserves much of its ancient character. It is now, called San Stefano in Rotondo, from its circular form; the thirty-four pillars, with arches springing from one to the other and intended to support the cupola, still remaining to prove its former magnificence.

113   This amphitheatre is the famous Colosseum begun by Trajan, and finished by Titus. It is needless to go into details respecting a building the gigantic ruins of which are so well known.

had been much reduced by the havoc made amongst them at several times, and was fallen into disrepute by neglect. Having expelled the most unworthy, he chose in their room the most honourable persons in Italy and the provinces. And to let it be known that those two orders differed not so much in privileges as in dignity, he declared publicly, when some altercation passed between a senator and a Roman knight, "that senators ought not to be treated with scurrilous language, unless they were the aggressors, and then it was fair and lawful to return it."

X. The business of the courts had prodigiously accumulated, partly from old law-suits which, on account of the interruption that had been given to the course of justice, still remained undecided, and partly from the accession of new suits arising out of the disorder of the times. He, therefore, chose commissioners by lot to provide for the restitution of what had been seized by violence during the war, and others with extraordinary jurisdiction to decide causes belonging to the centumviri, and reduce them to as small a number as possible, for the dispatch of which, otherwise, the lives of the litigants could scarcely allow sufficient time.

XI. Lust and luxury, from the licence which had long prevailed, had also grown to an enormous height. He, therefore, obtained a decree of the senate, that a woman who formed an union with the slave of another person, should be considered a bondwoman herself; and that usurers should not be allowed to take proceedings at law for the recovery of money lent to young men whilst they lived in their father's family, not even after their fathers were dead.

XII. In other affairs, from the beginning to the end of his government, he conducted himself with great moderation and clemency. He was so far from dissembling the obscurity of his extraction, that he frequently made mention of it himself. When some affected to trace his pedigree to the founders of Reate, and a companion of Hercules[114], whose monument is still to be seen on the Salarian road, he laughed at them for it. And he was so little fond of external and adventitious ornaments, that, on the day of his triumph[115], being quite tired of the length and tediousness of the procession, he could not forbear saying, "he was rightly served, for having in his old age been so silly as to desire a triumph; as if it was either due to

114   Hercules is said, after conquering Geryon in Spain, to have come into this part of Italy. One of his companions, the supposed founder of Reate, may have had the name of Flavus.

115   Vespasian and his son Titus had a joint triumph for the conquest of Judaea, which is described at length by Josephus, De Bell. Jud. vii. 16. The coins of Vespasian exhibiting the captive Judaea (Judaea capta), are probably familiar to the reader. See Harphrey's Coin Collector's Manual, p. 328.

his ancestors, or had ever been expected by himself." Nor would he for a long time accept of the tribunitian authority, or the title of Father of his Country. And in regard to the custom of searching those who came to salute him, he dropped it even in the time of the civil war.

XIII. He bore with great mildness the freedom used by his friends, the satirical allusions of advocates, and the petulance of philosophers. Licinius Mucianus, who had been guilty of notorious acts of lewdness, but, presuming upon his great services, treated him very rudely, he reproved only in private; and when complaining of his conduct to a common friend of theirs, he concluded with these words, "However, I am a man." Salvius Liberalis, in pleading the cause of a rich man under prosecution, presuming to say, "What is it to Caesar, if Hipparchus possesses a hundred millions of sesterces?" he commended him for it.

Demetrius, the Cynic philosopher[116], who had been sentenced to banishment, meeting him on the road, and refusing to rise up or salute him, nay, snarling at him in scurrilous language, he only called him a cur.

XIV. He was little disposed to keep up the memory of affronts or quarrels, nor did he harbour any resentment on account of them. He made a very splendid marriage for the daughter of his enemy Vitellius, and gave her, besides, a suitable fortune and equipage. Being in a great consternation after he was forbidden the court in the time of Nero, and asking those about him, what he should do? or, whither he should go? one of those whose office it was to introduce people to the emperor, thrusting him out,

---

116   Demetrius, who was born at Corinth, seems to have been a close imitator of Diogenes, the founder of the sect. Having come to Rome to study under Apollonius, he was banished to the islands, with other philosophers, by Vespasian.

bid him go to Morbonia[117]. But when this same person came afterwards to beg his pardon, he only vented his resentment in nearly the same words. He was so far from being influenced by suspicion or fear to seek the destruction of any one, that, when his friends advised him to beware of Metius Pomposianus, because it was commonly believed, on his nativity being cast, that he was destined by fate to the empire, he made him consul, promising for him, that he would not forget the benefit conferred.

XV. It will scarcely be found, that so much as one innocent person suffered in his

---

117   There being no such place as Morbonia, and the supposed name being derived from morbus, disease, some critics have supposed that Anticyra, the asylum of the incurables, (see CALIGULA, c. xxix.) is meant; but the probability is, that the expression used by the imperial chamberlain was only a courtly version of a phrase not very commonly adopted in the present day.

reign, unless in his absence, and without his knowledge, or, at least, contrary to his inclination, and when he was imposed upon. Although Helvidius Priscus[118] was the only man who presumed to salute him on his return from Syria by his private name of Vespasian, and, when he came to be praetor, omitted any mark of honour to him, or even any mention of him in his edicts, yet he was not angry, until Helvidius proceeded to inveigh against him with the most scurrilous language. Though he did indeed banish him, and afterwards ordered him to be put to death, yet he would gladly have saved him notwithstanding, and accordingly dispatched messengers to fetch back the executioners; and he would have saved him, had he not been deceived by a false account brought, that he had already perished. He never rejoiced at the death

118   Helvidius Priscus, a person of some celebrity as a philosopher and public man, is mentioned by Tacitus, Xiphilinus, and Arrian.

of any man; nay he would shed tears, and sigh, at the just punishment of the guilty.

XVI. The only thing deservedly blameable in his character was his love of money. For not satisfied with reviving the imposts which had been repealed in the time of Galba, he imposed new and onerous taxes, augmented the tribute of the provinces, and doubled that of some of them. He likewise openly engaged in a traffic, which is discreditable[119] even to a private individual, buying great quantities of goods, for the purpose of retailing them again to advantage. Nay, he made no scruple of selling the great offices of the state to candidates, and pardons to persons under prosecution, whether they were innocent or guilty. It is believed, that he advanced all the most rapacious amongst the procurators to higher offices, with the view of squeezing them after they had acquired great wealth. He was commonly said, "to have used them

---

119   Cicero speaks in strong terms of the sordidness of retail trade—Off. i. 24.

as sponges," because it was his practice, as we may say, to wet them when dry, and squeeze them when wet. It is said that he was naturally extremely covetous, and was upbraided with it by an old herdsman of his, who, upon the emperor's refusing to enfranchise him gratis, which on his advancement he humbly petitioned for, cried out, "That the fox changed his hair, but not his nature." On the other hand, some are of opinion, that he was urged to his rapacious proceedings by necessity, and the extreme poverty of the treasury and exchequer, of which he took public notice in the beginning of his reign; declaring that "no less than four hundred thousand millions of sesterces were wanting to carry on the government." This is the more likely to be true, because he applied to the best purposes what he procured by bad means.

XVII. His liberality, however, to all ranks of people, was excessive. He made up to several senators the estate required   by law to qualify them for that dignity; relieving likewise such men of consular rank as were poor, with a yearly allowance of five hundred thousand sesterces[120]; and rebuilt, in a better manner than before, several cities in different parts of the empire, which had been damaged by earthquakes or fires.

XVIII. He was a great encourager of learning and the liberal arts. He first granted to the Latin and Greek professors of rhetoric the yearly stipend of a hundred thousand

---

120   The sesterce being worth about two-pence half-penny of English money, the salary of a Roman senator was, in round numbers, five thousand pounds a year; and that of a professor, as stated in the succeeding chapter, one thousand pounds. From this scale, similar calculations may easily be made of the sums occurring in Suetonius's statements from time to time. There appears to be some mistake in the sum stated in c. xvi. just before, as the amount seems fabulous, whether it represented the floating debt, or the annual revenue, of the empire.

sesterces[121] each out of the exchequer. He also bought the freedom of superior poets and artists[122], and gave a noble gratuity to the restorer of the Coan of Venus[123], and to another artist who repaired the Colossus[124].

---

121   See AUGUSTUS, c. xliii. The proscenium of the ancient theatres was a solid erection of an architectural design, not shifted and varied as our stage-scenes.

122   Many eminent writers among the Romans were originally slaves, such as Terence and Phaedrus; and, still more, artists, physicians and artificers. Their talents procuring their manumission, they became the freedmen of their former masters. Vespasian, it appears from Suetonius, purchased the freedom of some persons of ability belonging to these classes.

123   The Coan Venus was the chef-d'oeuvre of Apelles, a native of the island of Cos, in the Archipelago, who flourished in the time of Alexander the Great. If it was the original painting which was now restored, it must have been well preserved.

124   Probably the colossal statue of Nero

Some one offering to convey some immense columns into the Capitol at a small expense by a mechanical contrivance, he rewarded him very handsomely for his invention, but would not accept his service, saying, "Suffer me to find maintenance for the poor people."[125]

XIX. In the games celebrated when the stage-scenery of the theatre of Marcellus[126] was repaired, he restored the old musical entertainments. He gave Apollinaris, the tragedian, four hundred thousand sesterces, and to Terpinus and Diodorus, the harpers, two hundred thousand; to some a hundred thousand; and the least he gave to any of the performers was forty thousand, besides many golden crowns.

(see his Life, c. xxxi.), afterwards placed in Vespasian's amphitheatre, which derived its name from it.

125   The usual argument in all times against the introduction of machinery.

126   See AUGUSTUS, c. xxix.

He entertained company constantly at his table, and often in great state and very sumptuously, in order to promote trade. As in the Saturnalia he made presents to the men which they were to carry away with them, so did he to the women upon the calends of March[127]; notwithstanding which, he could not wipe off the disrepute of his former stinginess. The Alexandrians called him constantly Cybiosactes; a name which had been given to one of their kings who was sordidly avaricious. Nay, at his funeral, Favo, the principal mimic, personating him, and imitating, as actors do, both his manner of speaking and his gestures, asked aloud of the procurators, "how much his funeral and the procession would cost?" And being

---

127   At the men's Saturnalia, a feast held in December attended with much revelling, the masters waited upon their slaves; and at the women's Saturnalia, held on the first of March, the women served their female attendants, by whom also they sent presents to their friends.

answered "ten millions of sesterces," he cried out, "give him but a hundred thousand sesterces, and they might throw his body into the Tiber, if they would."

XX. He was broad-set, strong-limbed, and his features gave the idea of a man in the act of straining himself. In consequence, one of the city wits, upon the emperor's desiring him "to say something droll respecting himself," facetiously answered, "I will, when you have done relieving your bowels."[128] He enjoyed a

---

128   Notwithstanding the splendour, and even, in many respects, the refinement of the imperial court, the language as well as the habits of the highest classes in Rome seem to have been but too commonly of the grossest description, and every scholar knows that many of their writers are not very delicate in their allusions. Apropos of the ludicrous account given in the text, Martial, on one occasion, uses still plainer language.

Utere lactucis, et mollibus utere malvis:

Nam faciem durum Phoebe, cacantis habes.–

iii. 89.

good state of health, though he used no other means to preserve it, than repeated friction, as much as he could bear, on his neck and other parts of his body, in the tennis-court attached to the baths, besides fasting one day in every month.

XXI. His method of life was commonly this. After he became emperor, he used to rise very early, often before daybreak. Having read over his letters, and the briefs of all the departments of the government offices; he admitted his friends; and while they were paying him their compliments, he would put on his own shoes, and dress himself with his own hands. Then, after the dispatch of such business as was brought before him, he rode out, and afterwards retired to repose, lying on his couch with one of his mistresses, of whom he kept several after the death of Caenis[129]. Coming out of his private apartments, he

---

129   See c. iii. and note.

passed to the bath, and then entered the supper-room. They say that he was never more good-humoured and indulgent than at that time: and therefore his attendants always seized that opportunity, when they had any favour to ask.

XXII. At supper, and, indeed, at other times, he was extremely free and jocose. For he had humour, but of a low kind, and he would sometimes use indecent language, such as is addressed to young girls about to be married. Yet there are some things related of him not void of ingenious pleasantry; amongst which are the following. Being once reminded by Mestrius Florus, that plaustra was a more proper expression than plostra, he the next day saluted him by the name of Flaurus[130].

---

130 Probably the emperor had not entirely worn off, or might even affect the rustic dialect of his Sabine countrymen; for among the peasantry the au was still pronounced o, as in plostrum for plaustrum, a waggon; and

A certain lady pretending to be desperately enamoured of him, he was prevailed upon to admit her to his bed; and after he had gratified her desires, he gave her[131] four hundred thousand sesterces. When his steward desired to know how he would have the sum entered in his accounts, he replied, "For Vespasian's being seduced."

XXIII. He used Greek verses very wittily; speaking of a tall man, who had enormous parts:

---

in orum for aurum, gold, etc. The emperor's retort was very happy, Flaurus being derived from a Greek word, which signifies worthless, while the consular critic's proper name, Florus, was connected with much more agreeable associations.

131   Some of the German critics think that the passage bears the sense of the gratuity having beer given by the lady, and that so parsimonious a prince as Vespasian was not likely to have paid such a sum as is here stated for a lady's proffered favours.

Makxi bibas, kradon dolichoskion enchos;
Still shaking, as he strode, his vast long spear.

And of Cerylus, a freedman, who being very rich, had begun to pass himself off as free-born, to elude the exchequer at his decease, and assumed the name of Laches, he said:

—O Lachaes, Lachaes,
Epan apothanaes, authis ex archaes esae Kaerylos.

Ah, Laches, Laches! when thou art no more,
Thou'lt Cerylus be called, just as before.

He chiefly affected wit upon his own shameful means of raising money, in order to wipe off the odium by some joke, and turn it into ridicule. One of his ministers, who was much in his favour, requesting of him a stewardship for some person, under pretence of his being his brother, he deferred granting him his petition, and in the meantime sent for the candidate, and having squeezed out of him as much money as he had agreed to give to his friend at court, he appointed him immediately to the office. The minister soon after renewing his application, "You must," said he, "find another brother; for the one you adopted is in truth mine."

Suspecting once, during a journey, that his mule-driver had alighted to shoe his mules, only in order to have an opportunity for allowing a person they met, who was engaged in a law-suit, to speak to him, he asked him, "how much he got for shoeing his mules?" and insisted on having a share of the profit. When his son Titus blamed him for even laying a tax upon urine, he applied to his nose a piece of the money he received in the first instalment, and asked him, "if it stunk?" And he replying no, "And yet," said he, "it is derived from urine."

Some deputies having come to acquaint him that a large statue, which would cost a vast sum, was ordered to be erected for him at the public expense, he told them to pay it down immediately, holding out the hollow of his hand, and saying, "there was a base ready for the statue." Not even when he was under the immediate apprehension and peril of death, could he forbear jesting. For when, among other prodigies, the mausoleum of the Caesars suddenly flew open, and a blazing star appeared in the heavens; one of the prodigies, he said, concerned Julia Calvina, who was of the family of Augustus[132]; and the other, the king of the Parthians, who wore his hair long. And when his distemper first seized

---

132 The Flavian family had their own tomb. See DOMITIAN, c. v. The prodigy, therefore, did not concern Vespasian. As to the tomb of the Julian family, see AUGUSTUS, c. ci.

him, "I suppose," said he, "I shall soon be a god."[133]

XXIV. In his ninth consulship, being seized, while in Campania, with a slight indisposition, and immediately returning to the city, he soon afterwards went thence to Cutiliae[134], and his estates in the country about Reate, where he used constantly to spend the summer. Here, though his disorder much increased, and he injured his bowels by too free use of the cold waters, he nevertheless attended to the dispatch of business, and even gave audience to

---

133 Alluding to the apotheosis of the emperors.

134 Cutiliae was a small lake, about three-quarters of a mile from Reate, now called Lago di Contigliano. It was very deep, and being fed from springs in the neighbouring hills, the water was exceedingly clear and cold, so that it was frequented by invalids, who required invigorating. Vespasian's paternal estates lay in the neighbourhood of Reate. See chap i.

ambassadors in bed. At last, being taken ill of a diarrhoea, to such a degree that he was ready to faint, he cried out, "An emperor ought to die standing upright." In endeavouring to rise, he died in the hands of those who were helping him up, upon the eighth of the calends of July [24th June][135], being sixty-nine years, one month, and seven days old.

XXV. All are agreed that he had such confidence in the calculations on his own nativity and that of his sons, that, after several conspiracies against him, he told the senate, that either his sons would succeed him, or nobody. It is said likewise, that he once saw in a dream a balance in the middle of the porch of the Palatine house exactly poised; in one scale of which stood Claudius and Nero, in the other, himself and his sons. The event corresponded to the symbol; for the reigns of the two parties

---

135   A.U.C. 832.

T. Flavius Vespasianus Augustus

were precisely of the same duration.[136]

* * * * * *

Neither consanguinity nor adoption, as formerly, but great influence in the army having now become the road to the imperial throne, no person could claim a better title to that elevation than Titus Flavius Vespasian. He had not only served with great reputation in the wars both in Britain and Judaea, but seemed as yet untainted with any vice which could pervert his conduct in the civil administration of the empire. It appears, however, that he was prompted more by the persuasion of friends, than by his own ambition, to prosecute the attainment of the imperial dignity. To render this enterprise more successful, recourse was had to a

---

136   Each dynasty lasted twenty-eight years. Claudius and Nero both reigning fourteen; and, of the Flavius family, Vespasian reigned ten, Titus three, and Domitian fifteen.

new and peculiar artifice, which, while well accommodated to the superstitious credulity of the Romans, impressed them with an idea, that Vespasian's destiny to the throne was confirmed by supernatural indications. But, after his elevation, we hear no more of his miraculous achievements.

The prosecution of the war in Britain, which had been suspended for some years, was resumed by Vespasian; and he sent thither Petilius Cerealis, who by his bravery extended the limits of the Roman province. Under Julius Frontinus, successor to that general, the invaders continued to make farther progress in the reduction of the island: but the commander who finally established the dominion of the Romans in Britain, was Julius Agricola, not less distinguished for his military achievements, than for his prudent regard to the civil administration of the country. He began his operations with the conquest of North Wales, whence passing over into the island of Anglesey, which had revolted since the time of Suetonius Paulinus, he again reduced it to subjection. Then proceeding northwards with his victorious army, he defeated the Britons in every engagement, took possession of all the territories in the southern parts of the island, and driving before him all who refused to submit to the Roman arms, penetrated even into the forests and mountains of Caledonia. He defeated the natives under Galgacus, their leader, in a decisive battle; and fixing a line of garrisons between the friths of Clyde and Forth, he secured the Roman province from the incursions of the people who occupied the parts of the island beyond that boundary. Wherever he established the Roman power, he introduced laws and civilization amongst the inhabitants, and employed every means of conciliating their affection, as well as of securing their obedience.

The war in Judaea, which had been

commenced under the former reign, was continued in that of Vespasian; but he left the siege of Jerusalem to be conducted by his son Titus, who displayed great valour and military talents in the prosecution of the enterprise. After an obstinate defence by the Jews, that city, so much celebrated in the sacred writings, was finally demolished, and the glorious temple itself, the admiration of the world, reduced to ashes; contrary, however, to the will of Titus, who exerted his utmost efforts to extinguish the flames.

The manners of the Romans had now attained to an enormous pitch of depravity, through the unbounded licentiousness of the tines; and, to the honour of Vespasian, he discovered great zeal in his endeavours to effect a national reformation. Vigilant, active, and persevering, he was indefatigable in the management of public affairs, and rose in the winter before day-break, to give audience to his officers of state. But if we give credit to the whimsical imposition of a tax upon urine, we cannot entertain any high opinion, either of his talents as a financier, or of the resources of the Roman empire. By his encouragement of science, he displayed a liberality, of which there occurs no example under all the preceding emperors, since the time of Augustus. Pliny the elder was now in the height of reputation, as well as in great favour with Vespasian; and it was probably owing not a little to the advice of that minister, that the emperor showed himself so much the patron of literary men. A writer mentioned frequently by Pliny, and who lived in this reign, was Licinius Mucianus, a Roman knight: he treated of the history and geography of the eastern countries. Juvenal, who had begun his Satires several years before, continued to inveigh against the flagrant vices of the times; but the only author whose writings we have to notice in the present reign, is a poet of a different class.

C. VALERIUS FLACCUS wrote a poem in eight books, on the Expedition of the Argonauts; a subject which, next to the wars of Thebes and Troy, was in ancient times the most celebrated. Of the life of this author, biographers have transmitted no particulars; but we may place his birth in the reign of Tiberius, before all the writers who flourished in the Augustan age were extinct. He enjoyed the rays of the setting sun which had illumined that glorious period, and he discovers the efforts of an ambition to recall its meridian splendour. As the poem was left incomplete by the death of the author, we can only judge imperfectly of the conduct and general consistency of the fable: but the most difficult part having been executed, without any room for the censure of candid criticism, we may presume that the sequel would have been finished with an equal claim to indulgence, if not to applause. The traditional anecdotes relative to the Argonautic expedition are introduced with propriety, and embellished with the graces of poetical fiction. In describing scenes of tenderness, this author is happily pathetic, and in the heat of combat, proportionably animated. His similes present the imagination with beautiful imagery, and not only illustrate, but give additional force to the subject. We find in Flaccus a few expressions not countenanced by the authority of the most celebrated Latin writers. His language, however, in general, is pure; but his words are perhaps not always the best that might have been chosen. The versification is elevated, though not uniformly harmonious; and there pervades the whole poem an epic dignity, which renders it superior to the production ascribed to Orpheus, or to that of Apollonius, on the same subject.

ELEVEN

Titus Flavius Vespasianus Augustus

I. TITUS, WHO HAD THE same cognomen with his father, was the darling and delight of mankind; so much did the natural genius, address, or good fortune he possessed tend to conciliate the favour of all. This was, indeed, extremely difficult, after he became emperor, as before that time, and even during the reign of his father, he lay under public odium and censure. He was born upon the third of the calends of January, [30th Dec.] in the year remarkable for the death of Caius[137], near the Septizonium[138], in a mean house, and a very small and dark room, which still exists, and is shown to the curious.

II. He was educated in the palace with Britannicus, and instructed in the same branches of learning, and under the same masters. During this time, they say, that a physiognomistbeingintroducedbyNarcissus,

---

137   Caligula. Titus was born A.U.C. 794; about A.D. 49.

138   The Septizonium was a circular building of seven stories. The remains of that of Septimus Severus, which stood on the side of the Palatine Hill, remained till the time of Pope Sixtus V., who removed it, and employed thirty-eight of its columns in ornamenting the church of St. Peter. It does not appear whether the Septizonium here mentioned as existing in the time of Titus, stood on the same spot.

the freedman of Claudius, to examine the features of Britannicus[139], positively affirmed that he would never become emperor, but that Titus, who stood by, would. They were so familiar, that Titus being next him at table, is thought to have tasted of the fatal potion which put an end to Britannicus's life, and to have contracted from it a distemper which hung about him a long time. In remembrance of all these circumstances, he afterwards erected a golden statue of him in the Palatium, and dedicated to him an equestrian statue of ivory; attending it in the Circensian procession, in which it is still carried to this day.

III. While yet a boy, he was remarkable for his noble endowments both of body and mind; and as he advanced in years, they became still more conspicuous. He had a fine person, combining an equal mixture of majesty and grace; was very strong, though

---

139   Britannicus, the son of Claudius and Messalina.

not tall, and somewhat corpulent. Gifted with an excellent memory, and a capacity for all the arts of peace and war; he was a perfect master of the use of arms and riding; very ready in the Latin and Greek tongues, both in verse and prose; and such was the facility he possessed in both, that he would harangue and versify extempore. Nor was he unacquainted with music, but could both sing and play upon the harp sweetly and scientifically. I have likewise been informed by many persons, that he was remarkably quick in writing short-hand, would in merriment and jest engage with his secretaries in the imitation of any hand-writing he saw, and often say, "that he was admirably qualified for forgery."

IV. He filled with distinction the rank of a military tribune both in Germany and Britain, in which he conducted himself with the utmost activity, and no less modesty and reputation; as appears evident from the great number of statues, with honourable inscriptions, erected to him in various parts of both those provinces. After serving in the wars, he frequented the courts of law, but with less assiduity than applause. About the same time, he married Arricidia, the daughter of Tertullus, who was only a knight, but had formerly been prefect of the pretorian guards. After her decease, he married Marcia Furnilla, of a very noble family, but afterwards divorced her, taking from her the daughter he had by her. Upon the expiration of his quaestorship, he was raised to the rank of commander of a legion[140], and took the two strong cities of Tarichaea and Gamala, in Judaea; and having his horse killed under him in a battle, he mounted another, whose rider he had encountered and slain.

V. Soon afterwards, when Galba came to be emperor, he was sent to congratulate him, and turned the eyes of all people

---

140   A.U.C. 820.

upon himself, wherever he came; it being the general opinion amongst them, that the emperor had sent for him with a design to adopt him for his son. But finding all things again in confusion, he turned back upon the road; and going to consult the oracle of Venus at Paphos about his voyage, he received assurances of obtaining the empire for himself. These hopes were speedily strengthened, and being left to finish the reduction of Judaea, in the final assault of Jerusalem, he slew seven of its defenders, with the like number of arrows, and took it upon his daughter's birth-day[141].

---

141 Jerusalem was taken, sacked, and burnt, by Titus, after a two years' siege, on the 8th September, A.U.C. 821, A.D. 69; it being the Sabbath. It was in the second year of the reign of Vespasian, when the emperor was sixty years old, and Titus himself, as he informs us, thirty. For particulars of the siege, see Josephus, De Bell. Jud. vi. and vii.; Hegesippus, Excid. Hierosol. v.; Dio, lxvi.; Tacitus, Hist. v.; Orosius, vii. 9.

So great was the joy and attachment of the soldiers, that, in their congratulations, they unanimously saluted him by the title of Emperor[142]; and, upon his quitting the province soon afterwards, would needs have detained him, earnestly begging him, and that not without threats, "either to stay, or take them all with him." This occurrence gave rise to the suspicion of his being engaged in a design to rebel against his father, and claim for himself the government of the East; and the suspicion increased, when, on his way to Alexandria, he wore a diadem at the consecration of the ox Apis at Memphis; and, though he did it only in compliance with an ancient religious usage of the country, yet there was some who put a bad construction upon it. Making, therefore, what haste he could into Italy, he arrived first at Rhegium, and sailing thence

---

142　For the sense in which Titus was saluted with the title of Emperor by the troops, see JULIUS CAESAR, c. lxxvi.

in a merchant ship to Puteoli, went to Rome with all possible expedition. Presenting himself unexpectedly to his father, he said, by way of contradicting the strange reports raised concerning him, "I am come, father, I am come."

VI. From that time he constantly acted as colleague with his father, and, indeed, as regent of the empire. He triumphed[143] with

-----

143 The joint triumph of Vespasian and Titus, which was celebrated A.U.C. 824, is fully described by Josephus, De Bell. Jud. vii. 24. It is commemorated by the triumphal monument called the Arch of Titus, erected by the senate and people of Rome after his death, and still standing at the foot of the Palatine Hill, on the road leading from the Colosseum to the Forum, and is one of the most beautiful as well as the most interesting models of Roman art. It consists of four stories of the three orders of architecture, the Corinthian being repeated in the two highest. Some of the bas-reliefs, still in good preservation, represent the table of the shew-bread, the seven-branched golden

his father, bore jointly with him the office of

---

candlestick, the vessel of incense, and the silver trumpets, which were taken by Titus from the Temple at Jerusalem, and, with the book of the law, the veil of the temple, and other spoils, were carried in the triumph. The fate of these sacred relics is rather interesting. Josephus says, that the veil and books of the law were deposited in the Palatium, and the rest of the spoils in the Temple of Peace. When that was burnt, in the reign of Commodus, these treasures were saved, and they were afterwards carried off by Genseric to Africa. Belisarius recovered them, and brought them to Constantinople, A.D. 520. Procopius informs us, that a Jew, who saw them, told an acquaintance of the emperor that it would not be advisable to carry them to the palace at Constantinople, as they could not remain anywhere else but where Solomon had placed them. This, he said, was the reason why Genseric had taken the Palace at Rome, and the Roman army had in turn taken that of the Vandal kings. Upon this, the emperor was so alarmed, that he sent the whole of them to the Christian churches at Jerusalem.

censor[144], and was, besides, his colleague not only in the tribunitian authority[145], but in seven consulships[146]. Taking upon himself the care and inspection of all offices, he dictated letters, wrote proclamations in his father's name, and pronounced his speeches in the senate in place of the quaestor. He likewise assumed the command of the pretorian guards, although no one but a Roman knight had ever before been their prefect. In this he conducted himself with great haughtiness and violence, taking off without scruple or delay all those he had most reason to suspect, after he had secretly sent his emissaries into the theatres and camp, to demand, as if by general consent, that the suspected persons should be delivered up to punishment. Among these, he invited to supper A. Caecina, a man of consular rank, whom he ordered to be stabbed at his

---

144   A.U.C. 825.
145   A.U.C. 824.
146   A.U.C. 823, 825, 827-830, 832.

departure, immediately after he had gone out of the room. To this act, indeed, he was provoked by an imminent danger; for he had discovered a writing under the hand of Caecina, containing an account of a plot hatched among the soldiers. By these acts, though he provided for his future security, yet for the present he so much incurred the hatred of the people, that scarcely ever any one came to the empire with a more odious character, or more universally disliked.

VII. Besides his cruelty, he lay under the suspicion of giving way to habits of luxury, as he often prolonged his revels till midnight with the most riotous of his acquaintance. Nor was he unsuspected of lewdness, on account of the swarms of catamites and eunuchs about him, and his well-known attachment to queen Berenice[147], who

147   Berenice, whose name is written by our author and others Beronice, was daughter of Agrippa the Great, who was by Aristobulus, grandson of Herod the Great. Having

been contracted to Mark, son of Alexander Lysimachus, he died before their union, and Agrippa married her to Herod, Mark's brother, for whom he had obtained from the emperor Claudius the kingdom of Chalcis. Herod also dying, Berenice, then a widow, lived with her brother, Agrippa, and was suspected of an incestuous intercourse with him. It was at this time that, on their way to the imperial court at Rome, they paid a visit to Festus, at Caesarea, and were present when St. Paul answered his accusers so eloquently before the tribunal of the governor. Her fascinations were so great, that, to shield herself from the charge of incest, she prevailed on Polemon, king of Cilicia, to submit to be circumcised, become a Jew, and marry her. That union also proving unfortunate, she appears to have returned to Jerusalem, and having attracted Vespasian by magnificent gifts, and the young Titus by her extraordinary beauty, she followed them to Rome, after the termination of the Jewish war, and had apartments in the palace, where she lived with Titus, "to all appearance, as his wife," as Xiphilinus informs us; and there seems no doubt that he would have married her, but for received from him, as it is reported, a promise of marriage. He was supposed, besides, to be of a rapacious disposition; for it is certain, that, in causes which came before his father, he used to offer his interest for sale, and take bribes. In short, people publicly expressed an unfavourable opinion of him, and said he would prove another Nero. This prejudice, however, turned out in the end to his advantage, and enhanced his praises to the highest pitch when he was found to possess no vicious propensities, but, on the contrary, the noblest virtues. His entertainments were agreeable rather than extravagant; and he surrounded himself with such excellent friends, that the succeeding princes adopted them as most serviceable to themselves and the state. He immediately sent away Berenice from the city, much against both their inclinations. Some of his old eunuchs,

---

the strong prejudices of the Romans against foreign alliances. Suetonius tells us with what pain they separated.

though such accomplished dancers, that they bore an uncontrollable sway upon the stage, he was so far from treating with any extraordinary kindness, that he would not so much as witness their performances in the crowded theatre. He violated no private right; and if ever man refrained from injustice, he did; nay, he would not accept of the allowable and customary offerings. Yet, in munificence, he was inferior to none of the princes before him. Having dedicated his amphitheatre[148], and built some warm baths[149] close by it

---

148   The Colosseum: it had been four years in building. See VESPAS. c. ix.

149   The Baths of Titus stood on the Esquiline Hill, on part of the ground which had been the gardens of Mecaenas. Considerable remains of them are still found among the vineyards; vaulted chambers of vast dimensions, some of which were decorated with arabesque paintings, still in good preservation. Titus appears to have erected a palace for himself adjoining; for the Laocoon, which is mentioned by Pliny as standing in this palace, was found

with great expedition, he entertained the people with most magnificent spectacles. He likewise exhibited a naval fight in the old Naumachia, besides a combat of gladiators; and in one day brought into the theatre five thousand wild beasts of all kinds.[150]

---

in the neighbouring ruins.

150   If the statements were not well attested, we might be incredulous as to the number of wild beasts collected for the spectacles to which the people of Rome were so passionately devoted. The earliest account we have of such an exhibition, was A.U.C. 502, when one hundred and forty-two elephants, taken in Sicily, were produced. Pliny, who gives this information, states that lions first appeared in any number, A.U.C. 652; but these were probably not turned loose. In 661, Sylla, when he was praetor, brought forward one hundred. In 696, besides lions, elephants, and bears, one hundred and fifty panthers were shown for the first time. At the dedication of Pompey's Theatre, there was the greatest exhibition of beasts ever then known; including seventeen

elephants, six hundred lions, which were killed in the course of five days, four hundred and ten panthers, etc. A rhinoceros also appeared for the first time. This was A.U.C. 701. The art of taming these beasts was carried to such perfection, that Mark Antony actually yoked them to his carriage. Julius Caesar, in his third dictatorship, A.U.C. 708, showed a vast number of wild beasts, among which were four hundred lions and a cameleopard. A tiger was exhibited for the first time at the dedication of the Theatre of Marcellus, A.U.C. 743. It was kept in a cage. Claudius afterwards exhibited four together. The exhibition of Titus, at the dedication of the Colosseum, here mentioned by Suetonius, seems to have been the largest ever made; Xiphilinus even adds to the number, and says, that including wild-boars, cranes, and other animals, no less than nine thousand were killed. In the reigns of succeeding emperors, a new feature was given to these spectacles, the Circus being converted into a temporary forest, by planting large trees, in which wild animals were turned loose, and the people were allowed to enter the wood and take what they pleased. In this instance, the game consisted principally

VIII. He was by nature extremely benevolent; for whereas all the emperors after Tiberius, according to the example he had set them, would not admit the grants made by former princes to be valid, unless they received their own sanction, he confirmed them all by one general edict, without waiting for any applications respecting them. Of all who petitioned for any favour, he sent none away without hopes. And when his ministers represented to him that he promised more than he could perform, he replied, "No one ought to go away downcast from an audience with his prince." Once at supper, reflecting that he had done nothing for any that day, he broke out into that memorable and justly-admired saying, "My friends, I have

---

of beasts of chase; and, on one occasion, one thousand stags, as many of the ibex, wild sheep (mouflions from Sardinia?), and other grazing animals, besides one thousand wild boars, and as many ostriches, were turned loose by the emperor Gordian.

lost a day."[151] More particularly, he treated
the people on all occasions with so much
courtesy, that, on his presenting them with a
show of gladiators, he declared, "He should
manage it, not according to his own fancy, but
that of the spectators," and did accordingly.
He denied them nothing, and very frankly
encouraged them to ask what they pleased.
Espousing the cause of the Thracian party
among the gladiators, he frequently joined in
the popular demonstrations in their favour,
but without compromising his dignity or doing
injustice. To omit no opportunity of acquiring
popularity, he sometimes made use himself
of the baths he had erected, without excluding
the common people. There happened in his
reign some dreadful accidents; an eruption
of Mount Vesuvius[152], in Campania, and a

---

151   "Diem perdidi." This memorable speech
is recorded by several other historians, and
praised by Eusebius in his Chronicles.
152   A.U.C. 832, A.D. 79. It is hardly
necessary to refer to the well-known Epistles

fire in Rome, which continued during three days and three nights[153]; besides a plague, such as was scarcely ever known before. Amidst these many great disasters, he not only manifested the concern which might be expected from a prince but even the affection of a father, for his people; one while comforting them by his proclamations, and another while relieving them to the utmost of his power. He chose by lot, from amongst the men of consular rank, commissioners

---

of Pliny the younger, vi. 16 and 20, giving an account of the first eruption of Vesuvius, in which Pliny, the historian, perished. And see hereafter, p. 475.

153   The great fire at Rome happened in the second year of the reign of Titus. It consumed a large portion of the city, and among the public buildings destroyed were the temples of Serapis and Isis, that of Neptune, the baths of Agrippa, the Septa, the theatres of Balbus and Pompey, the buildings and library of Augustus on the Palatine, and the temple of Jupiter in the Capitol.

Titus Flavius Vespasianus Augustus

for repairing the losses in Campania. The estates of those who had perished by the eruption of Vesuvius, and who had left no heirs, he applied to the repair of the ruined cities. With regard to the public buildings destroyed by fire in the City, he declared that nobody should be a loser but himself. Accordingly, he applied all the ornaments of his palaces to the decoration of the temples, and purposes of public utility, and appointed several men of the equestrian order to superintend the work. For the relief of the people during the plague, he employed, in the way of sacrifice and medicine, all means both human and divine. Amongst the calamities of the times, were informers and their agents; a tribe of miscreants who had grown up under the licence of former reigns. These he frequently ordered to be scourged or beaten with sticks in the Forum, and then, after he had obliged them to pass through the amphitheatre as a public spectacle, commanded them to be sold for slaves, or else banished them to some rocky islands. And to discourage such practices for the future, amongst other things, he prohibited actions to be successively brought under different laws for the same cause, or the state of affairs of deceased persons to be inquired into after a certain number of years.

IX. Having declared that he accepted the office of Pontifex Maximus for the purpose of preserving his hands undefiled, he faithfully adhered to his promise. For after that time he was neither directly nor indirectly concerned in the death of any person, though he sometimes was justly irritated. He swore "that he would perish himself, rather than prove the destruction of any man." Two men of patrician rank being convicted of aspiring to the empire, he only advised them to desist, saying, "that the sovereign power was disposed of by fate," and promised them, that if there was any thing else they desired of him, he would grant it. He also immediately sent messengers to the mother of one of them, who was at a great distance, and in deep anxiety about her son, to assure her of his safety. Nay, he not only invited them to sup with him, but next day, at a show of gladiators, purposely placed them close by him; and handed to them the arms of the combatants for his inspection. It is said likewise, that having had their nativities cast, he assured them, "that a great calamity was impending on both of them, but from another hand, and not from his." Though his brother was continually plotting against him, almost openly stirring up the armies to rebellion, and contriving to get away, yet he could not endure to put him to death, or to banish him from his presence; nor did he treat him with less respect than before. But from his first accession to the empire, he constantly declared him his partner in it, and that he should be his successor; begging of him sometimes in private, with tears in his eyes, "to return the affection he had for him."

X. Amidst all these favourable circumstances, he was cut off by an untimely death, more to the loss of mankind than himself. At the close of the public spectacles, he wept bitterly in the presence of the people, and then retired into the Sabine country[154], rather melancholy, because a victim had made its escape while he was sacrificing, and loud thunder had been heard while the atmosphere was serene. At the first resting-place on the road, he was seized with a fever, and being carried forward in a litter, they say that he drew back the curtains, and looked up to

---

154   See VESPASIAN, cc. i. and xxiv. The love of this emperor and his son Titus for the rural retirement of their paternal acres in the Sabine country, forms a striking contrast to the vicious attachment of such tyrants as Tiberius and Caligula for the luxurious scenes of Baiae, or the libidinous orgies of Capri.

heaven, complaining heavily, "that his life was taken from him, though he had done nothing to deserve it; for there was no action of his that he had occasion to repent of, but one." What that was, he neither disclosed himself, nor is it easy for us to conjecture. Some imagine that he alluded to the connection which he had formerly had with his brother's wife. But Domitia solemnly denied it on oath; which she would never have done, had there been any truth in the report; nay, she would certainly have gloried in it, as she was forward enough to boast of all her scandalous intrigues.

XI. He died in the same villa where his father had died before him, upon the Ides of September [the 13th of September]; two years, two months, and twenty days after he had succeeded his father; and in the one-and-fortieth year of his age[155]. As soon as the news of his death was published, all

---

155   A.U.C. 834, A.D. 82.

people mourned for him, as for the loss of some near relative. The senate assembled in haste, before they could be summoned by proclamation, and locking the doors of their house at first, but afterwards opening them, gave him such thanks, and heaped upon him such praises, now he was dead, as they never had done whilst he was alive and present amongst them.

*   *   *   *   *   *

TITUS FLAVIUS VESPASIAN, the younger, was the first prince who succeeded to the empire by hereditary right; and having constantly acted, after his return from Judaea, as colleague with his father in the administration, he seemed to be as well qualified by experience as he was by abilities, for conducting the affairs of the empire. But with respect to his natural disposition, and moral behaviour, the expectations entertained by the public were not equally flattering. He was immoderately addicted to luxury; he had betrayed a strong inclination to cruelty; and he lived in the habitual practice of lewdness, no less unnatural than intemperate. But, with a degree of virtuous resolution unexampled in history, he had no sooner taken into his hands the entire reins of government, than he renounced every vicious attachment. Instead of wallowing in luxury, as before, he became a model of temperance; instead of cruelty, he displayed the strongest proofs of humanity and benevolence; and in the room of lewdness, he exhibited a transition to the most unblemished chastity and virtue. In a word, so sudden and great a change was never known in the character of mortal; and he had the peculiar glory to receive the appellation of "the darling and delight of mankind."

Under a prince of such a disposition, the government of the empire could not but be conducted with the strictest regard to the public welfare. The reform, which was begun in the late reign, he prosecuted with the most ardent application; and, had he lived for a longer time, it is probable that his authority and example would have produced the most beneficial effects upon the manners of the Romans.

During the reign of this emperor, in the seventy-ninth year of the Christian era, happened the first eruption of Mount Vesuvius, which has ever since been celebrated for its volcano. Before this time, Vesuvius is spoken of, by ancient writers, as being covered with orchards and vineyards, and of which the middle was dry and barren. The eruption was accompanied by an earthquake, which destroyed several cities of Campania, particularly Pompeii and Herculaneum; while the lava, pouring down the mountain in torrents, overwhelmed, in various directions, the adjacent plains. The burning ashes were carried not only over the neighbouring country, but as far as the shores of Egypt, Libya, and even Syria. Amongst those to whom this dreadful eruption proved fatal, was Pliny, the celebrated naturalist, whose curiosity to examine the phenomenon led him so far within the verge of danger, that he could not afterwards escape.

PLINY, surnamed the Elder, was born at Verona, of a noble family. He distinguished himself early by his military achievements in the German war, received the dignity of an Augur, at Rome, and was afterwards appointed governor of Spain. In every public character, he acquitted himself with great reputation, and enjoyed the esteem of the several emperors under whom he lived. The assiduity with which he applied himself to the collection of information, either curious or useful, surpasses all example. From an early hour in the morning, until late at night, he was almost constantly employed in discharging the duties of his public station, in reading or hearing books read by his amanuensis, and in extracting from them whatever seemed worthy of notice. Even during his meals, and while travelling in his carriage upon business, he prosecuted with unremitting zeal and diligence his taste for enquiry and compilation. No man ever displayed so strong a persuasion of the value of time, or availed himself so industriously of it. He considered every moment as lost which was not employed in literary pursuits. The books which he wrote, in consequence of this indefatigable exertion, were, according to the account transmitted by his nephew, Pliny the younger, numerous, and on various subjects. The catalogue of them is as follows: a book on Equestrian Archery, which discovered much skill in the art; the Life of Q. Pomponius Secundus; twenty books of the Wars of Germany; a complete treatise on the Education of an Orator, in six volumes; eight books of Doubtful Discourses, written in the latter part of the reign of Nero, when every kind of moral discussion was attended with danger; with a hundred and sixty volumes of remarks on the writings of the various authors which he had perused. For the last-mentioned production only, and before it was brought near to its accomplishment, we are told, that he was offered by Largius Licinius four hundred thousand sesterces, amounting to upwards of three thousand two hundred pounds sterling; an enormous sum for the copyright of a book before the invention of printing! But the only surviving work of this voluminous author is his Natural History, in thirty-seven books, compiled from the various writers who had treated of that extensive and interesting subject.

If we estimate this great work either by the authenticity of the information which it contains, or its utility in promoting the advancement of arts and sciences, we should not consider it as an object of any extraordinary encomiums; but when we view it as a literary monument, which displays the whole knowledge of the ancients, relative to

Natural History, collected during a period of about seven hundred years, from the time of Thales the Milesian, it has a just claim to the attention of every speculative enquirer. It is not surprising, that the progress of the human mind, which, in moral science, after the first dawn of enquiry, was rapid both amongst the Greeks and Romans, should be slow in the improvement of such branches of knowledge as depended entirely on observation and facts, which were peculiarly difficult of attainment. Natural knowledge can only be brought to perfection by the prosecution of enquiries in different climates, and by a communication of discoveries amongst those by whom it is cultivated. But neither could enquiries be prosecuted, nor discoveries communicated, with success, while the greater part of the world was involved in barbarism, while navigation was slow and limited, and the art of printing unknown. The consideration of these circumstances will afford sufficient apology for the imperfect state in which natural science existed amongst the ancients. But we proceed to give an abstract of their extent, as they appear in the compilation of Pliny.

This work is divided into thirty-seven books; the first of which contains the Preface, addressed to the emperor Vespasian, probably the father, to whom the author pays high compliments. The second book treats of the world, the elements, and the stars. In respect to the world, or rather the universe, the author's opinion is the same with that of several ancient philosophers, that it is a Deity, uncreated, infinite, and eternal. Their notions, however, as might be expected, on a subject so incomprehensible, are vague, confused, and imperfect. In a subsequent chapter of the same book, where the nature of the Deity is more particularly considered, the author's conceptions of infinite power are so inadequate, that, by way of consolation for the limited powers of man, he observes that there are many things even beyond the power of the Supreme Being; such, for instance, as the annihilation of his own existence; to which the author adds, the power of rendering mortals eternal, and of raising the dead. It deserves to be remarked, that, though a future state of rewards and punishments was maintained by the most eminent among the ancient philosophers, the resurrection of the body was a doctrine with which they were wholly unacquainted.

The author next treats of the planets, and the periods of their respective revolutions; of the stars, comets, winds, thunder, lightning, and other natural phenomena, concerning all which he delivers the hypothetical notions maintained by the ancients, and mentions a variety of extraordinary incidents which had occurred in different parts of the world. The third book contains a general system of geography, which is continued through the fourth, fifth, and sixth books. The seventh treats of conception, and the generation of the human species, with a number of miscellaneous observations, unconnected with the general subject. The eighth treats of quadrupeds; the ninth, of aquatic animals; the tenth, of birds; the eleventh, of insects and reptiles; the twelfth, of trees; the thirteenth, of ointments, and of trees which grow near the sea-coast; the fourteenth, of vines; the fifteenth, of fruit-trees; the sixteenth, of forest-trees; the seventeenth, of the cultivation of trees; the eighteenth, of agriculture; the nineteenth, of the nature of lint, hemp, and similar productions; the twentieth, of the medicinal qualities of vegetables cultivated in gardens; the twenty-first, of flowers; the twenty-second, of the properties of herbs; the twenty-third, of the medicines yielded by cultivated trees; the twenty-fourth, of medicines derived from forest-trees; the twenty-fifth, of the properties of wild herbs, and the origin of their use; the twenty-sixth, of other remedies for diseases, and of some new diseases; the twenty-seventh, of different kinds of herbs; the twenty-eighth, twenty-ninth, and thirtieth, of medicines procured from animals; the thirty-first and thirty-second, of medicines obtained from aquatic animals, with some extraordinary facts relative to the subject; the thirty-third, of the nature of metals; the thirty-fourth, of brass, iron, lead, and tin; the thirty-fifth, of pictures, and observations relative to painting; the thirty-sixth, of the nature of stones and marbles; the thirty-seventh, of the origin of gems. To the contents of each book, the author subjoins a list of the writers from whom his observations have been collected.

Of Pliny's talents as a writer, it might be deemed presumptuous to form a decided opinion from his Natural History, which is avowedly a compilation from various authors, and executed with greater regard to the matter of the work, than to the elegance of composition. Making allowance, however, for a degree of credulity, common to the human mind in the early stage of physical researches, he is far from being deficient in the essential qualifications of a writer of Natural History. His descriptions appear to be accurate, his observations precise, his narrative is in general perspicuous, and he often illustrates his subject by a vivacity of thought, as well as by a happy turn of expression. It has been equally his endeavour to give novelty to stale disquisitions, and authority to new observations. He has both removed the rust, and dispelled the obscurity, which enveloped the doctrines of many ancient naturalists; but, with all his care and industry, he has exploded fewer errors, and sanctioned a greater number of doubtful opinions, than was consistent with the exercise of unprejudiced and severe investigation.

Pliny was fifty-six years of age at the time of his death; the manner of which is accurately related by his nephew, the elegant Pliny the Younger, in a letter to Tacitus, who entertained a design of writing the life of the naturalist.

TWELVE

Titus Flavius Domitianus

I. DOMITIAN WAS BORN UPON the ninth of the calends of November [24th October][156], when his father was consul elect, (being to enter upon his office the month following,) in the sixth region of the city, at the Pomegranate[157], in the

---

156 A.U.C. 804.

157 A street, in the sixth region of Rome, so called, probably, from a remarkable specimen

house which he afterwards converted into a temple of the Flavian family. He is said to have spent the time of his youth in so much want and infamy, that he had not one piece of plate belonging to him; and it is well known, that Clodius Pollio, a man of pretorian rank, against whom there is a poem of Nero's extant, entitled Luscio, kept a note in his hand-writing, which he sometimes produced, in which Domitian made an assignation with him for the foulest purposes. Some, likewise, have said, that he prostituted himself to Nerva, who succeeded him. In the war with Vitellius, he fled into the Capitol with his uncle Sabinus, and a part of the troops they had in the city[158]. But the enemy breaking in, and the temple being set on fire, he hid himself all night with the sacristan; and next morning, assuming the disguise of a worshipper of

of this beautiful shrub which had made free growth on the spot.
158   VITELLIUS, c. xv.

Isis, and mixing with the priests of that idle superstition, he got over the Tiber[159], with only one attendant, to the house of a woman who was the mother of one of his school-fellows, and lurked there so close, that, though the enemy, who were at his heels, searched very strictly after him, they could not discover him. At last, after the success of his party, appearing in public, and being unanimously saluted by the title of Caesar, he assumed the office of praetor of the City, with consular authority, but in fact had nothing but the name; for the jurisdiction he transferred to his next colleague. He used, however, his absolute power so licentiously, that even then he plainly discovered what sort of prince he was likely to prove. Not to go into details, after he had made free with the wives of many men of distinction, he took

---

159   Tacitus (Hist. iii.) differs from Suetonius, saying that Domitian took refuge with a client of his father's near the Velabrum. Perhaps he found it more safe afterwards to cross the Tiber.

Domitia Longina from her husband, Aelias Lamia, and married her; and in one day disposed of above twenty offices in the city and the provinces; upon which Vespasian said several times, "he wondered he did not send him a successor too."

II. He likewise designed an expedition into Gaul and Germany[160], without the least necessity for it, and contrary to the advice of all his father's friends; and this he did only with the view of equalling his brother in military achievements and glory. But for this he was severely reprimanded, and that he might the more effectually be reminded of his age and position, was made to live with his father, and his litter had to follow his father's and brother's carriage, as often as they went abroad; but he attended them in their triumph for

---

160   One of Domitian's coins bears on the reverse a captive female and soldier, with GERMANIA DEVICTA.

the conquest of Judaea[161], mounted on a white horse. Of the six consulships which he held, only one was ordinary; and that he obtained by the cession and interest of his brother. He greatly affected a modest behaviour, and, above all, a taste for poetry; insomuch, that he rehearsed his performances in public, though it was an art he had formerly little cultivated, and which he afterwards despised and abandoned. Devoted, however, as he was at this time to poetical pursuits, yet when Vologesus, king of the Parthians, desired succours against the Alani, with one of Vespasian's sons to command them, he laboured hard to procure for himself that appointment. But the scheme proving abortive, he endeavoured by presents and promises to engage other kings of the East to make a similar request. After his father's death, he was for some time in doubt, whether

---

161   VESPASIAN, c. xii; TITUS, c. vi.

he should not offer the soldiers a donative double to that of his brother, and made no scruple of saying frequently, "that he had been left his partner in the empire, but that his father's will had been fraudulently set aside." From that time forward, he was constantly engaged in plots against his brother, both publicly and privately; until, falling dangerously ill, he ordered all his attendants to leave him, under pretence of his being dead, before he really was so; and, at his decease, paid him no other honour than that of enrolling him amongst the gods; and he often, both in speeches and edicts, carped at his memory by sneers and insinuations.

III. In the beginning of his reign, he used to spend daily an hour by himself in private, during which time he did nothing else but catch flies, and stick them through the body with a sharp pin. When some one therefore inquired, "whether any one was with the emperor," it was significantly answered by

Vibius Crispus, "Not so much as a fly." Soon after his advancement, his wife Domitia, by whom he had a son in his second consulship, and whom the year following he complimented with the title of Augusta, being desperately in love with Paris, the actor, he put her away; but within a short time afterwards, being unable to bear the separation, he took her again, under pretence of complying with the people's importunity. During some time, there was in his administration a strange mixture of virtue and vice, until at last his virtues themselves degenerated into vices; being, as we may reasonably conjecture concerning his character, inclined to avarice through want, and to cruelty through fear.

IV. He frequently entertained the people with most magnificent and costly shows, not only in the amphitheatre, but the circus; where, besides the usual races with chariots drawn by two or four horses a-breast, he exhibited the representation of an engagement between both horse and foot, and a sea-fight in the amphitheatre. The people were also entertained with the chase of wild beasts and the combat of gladiators, even in the night-time, by torch-light. Nor did men only fight in these spectacles, but women also. He constantly attended at the games given by the quaestors, which had been disused for some time, but were revived by him; and upon those occasions, always gave the people the liberty of demanding two pair of gladiators out of his own school, who appeared last in court uniforms. Whenever he attended the shows of gladiators, there stood at his feet a little boy dressed in scarlet, with a prodigiously small head, with whom he used to talk very much, and sometimes seriously. We are assured, that he was overheard asking him, "if he knew for what reason he had in the late appointment, made Metius Rufus governor of Egypt?" He presented the people with naval fights, performed by fleets almost as numerous as those usually employed in real engagements; making a vast lake near the Tiber[162], and building seats round it. And he witnessed them himself during a very heavy rain. He likewise celebrated the Secular games[163], reckoning not from the year in which they had been exhibited by Claudius, but from the time of Augustus's celebration of them. In these, upon the day of the Circensian sports, in order to have a hundred races performed, he reduced each course from seven rounds to five. He likewise instituted, in honour of Jupiter Capitolinus, a solemn contest in music to be performed every five years; besides horse-racing and

---

162   Such excavations had been made by Julius and by Augustus (AUG. xliii.), and the seats for the spectators fitted up with timber in a rude way. That was on the other side of the Tiber. The Naumachia of Domitian occupies the site of the present Piazza d'Espagna, and was larger and more ornamented.

163   A.U.C. 841. See AUGUSTUS, c. xxxi.

gymnastic exercises, with more prizes than are at present allowed. There was also a public performance in elocution, both Greek and Latin and besides the musicians who sung to the harp, there were others who played concerted pieces or solos, without vocal accompaniment. Young girls also ran races in the Stadium, at which he presided in his sandals, dressed in a purple robe, made after the Grecian fashion, and wearing upon his head a golden crown bearing the effigies of Jupiter, Juno, and Minerva; with the flamen of Jupiter, and the college of priests sitting by his side in the same dress; excepting only that their crowns had also his own image on them. He celebrated also upon the Alban mount every year the festival of Minerva, for whom he had appointed a college of priests, out of which were chosen by lot persons to preside as governors over the college; who were obliged to entertain the people with extraordinary chases of wild-beasts, and stage-plays, besides contests for prizes in oratory and poetry. He thrice bestowed upon the people a largess of three hundred sesterces each man; and, at a public show of gladiators, a very plentiful feast. At the festival of the Seven Hills[164], he distributed large hampers of provisions to the senatorian and equestrian orders, and small baskets to the common people, and encouraged them to eat by setting them the example. The day after, he scattered among the people a variety of cakes and other delicacies to be scrambled for; and on the greater part of them falling amidst the seats of the crowd, he ordered five hundred tickets to be thrown into each range of benches belonging to the senatorian and equestrian orders.

V. He rebuilt many noble edifices which had been destroyed by fire, and amongst them

---

164   This feast was held in December. Plutarch informs us that it was instituted in commemoration of the seventh hill being included in the city bounds.

the Capitol, which had been burnt down a second time[165]; but all the inscriptions were in his own name, without the least mention of the original founders. He likewise erected a new temple in the Capitol to Jupiter Custos, and a forum, which is now called Nerva's[166],

---

165   The Capitol had been burnt, for the third time, in the great fire mentioned TITUS, c. viii. The first fire happened in the Marian war, after which it was rebuilt by Pompey, the second in the reign of Vitellius.

166   This forum, commenced by Domitian and completed by Nerva, adjoined the Roman Forum and that of Augustus, mentioned in c. xxix. of his life. From its communicating with the two others, it was called Transitorium. Part of the wall which bounded it still remains, of a great height, and 144 paces long. It is composed of square masses of freestone, very large, and without any cement; and it is not carried in a straight line, but makes three or four angles, as if some buildings had interfered with its direction.

as also the temple of the Flavian family[167], a stadium[168], an odeum[169], and a naumachia[170]; out of the stone dug from which, the sides of the Circus Maximus, which had been burnt down, were rebuilt.

VI. He undertook several expeditions, some from choice, and some from necessity. That against the Catti[171] was unprovoked, but that against the Sarmatians was necessary; an entire legion, with its commander, having been cut off by them. He sent two expeditions against the Dacians; the first upon the defeat of Oppius Sabinus, a man

---

167   The residence of the Flavian family was converted into a temple. See c. i. of the present book.

168   The Stadium was in the shape of a circus, and used for races both of men and horses.

169   The Odeum was a building intended for musical performances. There were four of them at Rome.

170   See before, c. iv.

171   See VESPASIAN, c. xiv.

of consular rank; and the other, upon that of Cornelius Fuscus, prefect of the pretorian cohorts, to whom he had entrusted the conduct of that war. After several battles with the Catti and Daci, he celebrated a double triumph. But for his successes against the Sarmatians, he only bore in procession the laurel crown to Jupiter Capitolinus. The civil war, begun by Lucius Antonius, governor of Upper Germany, he quelled, without being obliged to be personally present at it, with remarkable good fortune. For, at the very moment of joining battle, the Rhine suddenly thawing, the troops of the barbarians which were ready to join L. Antonius, were prevented from crossing the river. Of this victory he had notice by some presages, before the messengers who brought the news of it arrived. For upon the very day the battle was fought, a splendid eagle spread its wings round his statue at Rome, making most joyful cries. And shortly after, a rumour became common, that Antonius was slain; nay, many positively affirmed, that they saw his head brought to the city.

VII. He made many innovations in common practices. He abolished the Sportula[172], and revived the old practice of regular suppers. To the four former parties in the Circensian games, he added two new, who were gold and scarlet. He prohibited the players from acting in the theatre, but permitted them the practice of their art in private houses. He forbad the castration of males; and reduced the price of the eunuchs who were still left in the hands of the dealers in slaves. On the occasion of a great abundance of wine, accompanied by a scarcity of corn, supposing that the tillage of the ground was neglected for the sake of attending too much to the cultivation of vineyards, he published a proclamation forbidding the planting of any new vines in Italy, and

---

172   See NERD, c. xvi.

ordering the vines in the provinces to be cut down, nowhere permitting more than one half of them to remain[173]. But he did not persist in the execution of this project. Some of the greatest offices he conferred upon his freedmen and soldiers. He forbad two legions to be quartered in the same camp, and more than a thousand sesterces to be deposited by any soldier with the standards; because it was thought that Lucius Antonius had been encouraged in his late project by the large sum deposited in the military chest by the two legions which he had in the same winter-quarters. He made an addition to the soldiers' pay, of three gold pieces a year.

VIII. In the administration of justice he was diligent and assiduous; and frequently sat in the Forum out of course, to cancel the judgments of the court of The One Hundred, which had been procured through favour,

---

173   This absurd edict was speedily revoked. See afterwards c. xiv.

or interest. He occasionally cautioned the judges of the court of recovery to beware of being too ready to admit claims for freedom brought before them. He set a mark of infamy upon judges who were convicted of taking bribes, as well as upon their assessors. He likewise instigated the tribunes of the people to prosecute a corrupt aedile for extortion, and to desire the senate to appoint judges for his trial. He likewise took such effectual care in punishing magistrates of the city, and governors of provinces, guilty of malversation, that they never were at any time more moderate or more just. Most of these, since his reign, we have seen prosecuted for crimes of various kinds. Having taken upon himself the reformation of the public manners, he restrained the licence of the populace in sitting promiscuously with the knights in the theatre. Scandalous libels, published to defame persons of rank, of either sex, he suppressed, and inflicted upon their authors a mark of infamy. He expelled a man of quaestorian rank from the senate, for practising mimicry and dancing. He debarred infamous women the use of litters; as also the right of receiving legacies, or inheriting estates. He struck out of the list of judges a Roman knight for taking again his wife whom he had divorced and prosecuted for adultery. He condemned several men of the senatorian and equestrian orders, upon the Scantinian law[174]. The lewdness of the Vestal Virgins, which had been overlooked by his father and brother, he punished severely, but in different ways; viz. offences committed before his reign, with death, and those since its commencement, according to ancient custom. For to the two sisters called Ocellatae, he gave liberty to choose the mode of death which they preferred, and

---

174   This was an ancient law levelled against adultery and other pollutions, named from its author Caius Scatinius, a tribune of the people. There was a Julian law, with the same object. See AUGUSTUS, c. xxxiv.

banished their paramours. But Cornelia, the president of the Vestals, who had formerly been acquitted upon a charge of incontinence, being a long time after again prosecuted and condemned, he ordered to be buried alive; and her gallants to be whipped to death with rods in the Comitium; excepting only a man of praetorian rank, to whom, because he confessed the fact, while the case was dubious, and it was not established against him, though the witnesses had been put to the torture, he granted the favour of banishment. And to preserve pure and undefiled the reverence due to the gods, he ordered the soldiers to demolish a tomb, which one of his freedmen had erected for his son out of the stones designed for the temple of Jupiter Capitolinus, and to sink in the sea the bones and relics buried in it.

IX. Upon his first succeeding to power, he felt such an abhorrence for the shedding of blood, that, before his father's arrival in

Rome, calling to mind the verse of Virgil,
Impia quam caesis gens est epulata juvencis,[175]

Ere impious man, restrain'd from blood in vain,
Began to feast on flesh of bullocks slain,

he designed to have published a proclamation, "to forbid the sacrifice of oxen." Before his accession to the imperial authority, and during some time afterwards, he scarcely ever gave the least grounds for being suspected of covetousness or avarice; but, on the contrary, he often afforded proofs, not only of his justice, but his liberality. To all about him he was generous even to profusion, and recommended nothing more earnestly to them than to avoid doing anything mean. He would not accept the

---

175   Geor. xi. 537.

property left him by those who had children. He also set aside a legacy bequeathed by the will of Ruscus Caepio, who had ordered "his heir to make a present yearly to each of the senators upon their first assembling." He exonerated all those who had been under prosecution from the treasury for above five years before; and would not suffer suits to be renewed, unless it was done within a year, and on condition, that the prosecutor should be banished, if he could not make good his cause. The secretaries of the quaestors having engaged in trade, according to custom, but contrary to the Clodian law[176], he pardoned them for what was past. Such portions of land as had been left when it was divided amongst the veteran soldiers, he granted to the ancient possessors, as belonging to then by prescription. He put a stop to false prosecutions in the exchequer, by severely punishing the prosecutors; and

---

176   See Livy, xxi. 63, and Cicero against Verres, v. 18.

this saying of his was much taken notice of "that a prince who does not punish informers, encourages them."

X. But he did not long persevere in this course of clemency and justice, although he sooner fell into cruelty than into avarice. He put to death a scholar of Paris, the pantomimic[177], though a minor, and then sick, only because, both in person and the practice of his art, he resembled his master; as he did likewise Hermogenes of Tarsus for some oblique reflections in his History; crucifying, besides, the scribes who had copied the work. One who was master of a band of gladiators, happening to say, "that a Thrax was a match for a Marmillo[178], but not so for the exhibitor of the games", he ordered him to be dragged from the benches into the arena, and exposed to the dogs, with this label upon him, "A Parmularian[179]

---

177   See VESPASIAN, c. iii.
178   Cant names for gladiators.
179   The faction which favoured the "Thrax"

guilty of talking impiously." He put to death many senators, and amongst them several men of consular rank. In this number were, Civica Cerealis, when he was proconsul in Africa, Salvidienus Orfitus, and Acilius Glabrio in exile, under the pretence of their planning to revolt against him. The rest he punished upon very trivial occasions; as Aelius Lamia for some jocular expressions, which were of old date, and perfectly harmless; because, upon his commending his voice after he had taken his wife from him[180], he replied, "Alas! I hold my tongue." And when Titus advised him to take another wife, he answered him thus: "What! have you a mind to marry?" Salvius Cocceianus was condemned to death for keeping the birth-day of his uncle Otho, the emperor: Metius Pomposianus, because he was commonly reported to have an imperial

---

party.
180   DOMITIAN, c. i.

nativity[181], and to carry about with him a map of the world upon vellum, with the speeches of kings and generals extracted out of Titus Livius; and for giving his slaves the names of Mago and Hannibal; Sallustius Lucullus, lieutenant in Britain, for suffering some lances of a new invention to be called "Lucullean;" and Junius Rusticus, for publishing a treatise in praise of Paetus Thrasea and Helvidius Priscus, and calling them both "most upright men." Upon this occasion, he likewise banished all the philosophers from the city and Italy. He put to death the younger Helvidius, for writing a farce, in which, under the character of Paris and Oenone, he reflected upon his having divorced his wife; and also Flavius Sabinus, one of his cousins, because, upon his being chosen at the consular election to that office, the public crier had, by a blunder, proclaimed him to the people

---

181   See VESPASIAN, c. xiv.

not consul, but emperor. Becoming still more savage after his success in the civil war, he employed the utmost industry to discover those of the adverse party who absconded: many of them he racked with a new-invented torture, inserting fire through their private parts; and from some he cut off their hands. It is certain, that only two of any note were pardoned, a tribune who wore the narrow stripe, and a centurion; who, to clear themselves from the charge of being concerned in any rebellious project, proved themselves to have been guilty of prostitution, and consequently incapable of exercising any influence either over the general or the soldiers.

XI. His cruelties were not only excessive, but subtle and unexpected. The day before he crucified a collector of his rents, he sent for him into his bed-chamber, made him sit down upon the bed by him, and sent him away well pleased, and, so far as could be inferred from his treatment, in a state of perfect security; having vouchsafed him the favour of a plate of meat from his own table. When he was on the point of condemning to death Aretinus Clemens, a man of consular rank, and one of his friends and emissaries, he retained him about his person in the same or greater favour than ever; until at last, as they were riding together in the same litter, upon seeing the man who had informed against him, he said, "Are you willing that we should hear this base slave tomorrow?" Contemptuously abusing the patience of men, he never pronounced a severe sentence without prefacing it with words which gave hopes of mercy; so that, at last, there was not a more certain token of a fatal conclusion, than a mild commencement. He brought before the senate some persona accused of treason, declaring, "that he should prove that day how dear he was to the senate;" and so influenced them, that they condemned the accused to be punished according to the ancient usage[182]. Then, as if alarmed at the extreme severity of their punishment, to lessen the odiousness of the proceeding, he interposed in these words; for it is not foreign to the purpose to give them precisely as they were delivered: "Permit me, Conscript Fathers, so far to prevail upon your affection for me, however extraordinary the request may seem, as to grant the condemned criminals the favour of dying in the manner they choose. For by so doing, ye will spare your own eyes, and the world will understand that I interceded with the senate on their behalf."

XII. Having exhausted the exchequer by the expense of his buildings and public spectacles, with the augmentation of pay lately granted to the troops, he made an attempt at the reduction of the army, in order to lessen the military charges. But reflecting, that he should, by this measure, expose

---

182   This cruel punishment is described in NERO, c. xlix.

himself to the insults of the barbarians, while it would not suffice to extricate him from his embarrassments, he had recourse to plundering his subjects by every mode of exaction. The estates of the living and the dead were sequestered upon any accusation, by whomsoever preferred. The unsupported allegation of any one person, relative to a word or action construed to affect the dignity of the emperor, was sufficient. Inheritances, to which he had not the slightest pretension, were confiscated, if there was found so much as one person to say, he had heard from the deceased when living, "that he had made the emperor his heir." Besides the exactions from others, the poll-tax on the Jews was levied with extreme rigour, both on those who lived after the manner of Jews in the city, without publicly professing themselves to be such[183], and

---

183   Gentiles who were proselytes to the Jewish religion; or, perhaps, members of the Christian sect, who were confounded with

on those who, by concealing their origin, avoided paying the tribute imposed upon that people. I remember, when I was a youth, to have been present[184], when an old man, ninety years of age, had his person exposed to view in a very crowded court, in order that, on inspection, the procurator might satisfy himself whether he was circumcised.[185]

From his earliest years Domitian was any thing but courteous, of a forward, assuming disposition, and extravagant both in his words and actions. When Caenis, his father's concubine, upon her return from Istria,

---

them. See the note to TIBERIUS, c. xxxvi. The tax levied on the Jews was two drachmas per head. It was general throughout the empire.

184   We have had Suetonius's reminiscences, derived through his grandfather and father successively, CALIGULA, c. xix.; OTHO, c. x. We now come to his own, commencing from an early age.

185   This is what Martial calls, "Mentula tributis damnata."

offered him a kiss, as she had been used to do, he presented her his hand to kiss. Being indignant, that his brother's son-in-law should be waited on by servants dressed in white[186], he exclaimed,

ouk agathon polykoiraniae.[187]
Too many princes are not good.

XIII. After he became emperor, he had the assurance to boast in the senate, "that he had bestowed the empire on his father and brother, and they had restored it to him." And upon taking his wife again, after the divorce, he declared by proclamation, "that he had recalled her to his pulvinar."[188] He was not a

---

186   The imperial liveries were white and gold.
187   See CALIGULA, c. xxi., where the rest of the line is quoted; eis koiranos esto.
188   An assumption of divinity, as the pulvinar was the consecrated bed, on which the images of the gods reposed.

little pleased too, at hearing the acclamations of the people in the amphitheatre on a day of festival, "All happiness to our lord and lady." But when, during the celebration of the Capitoline trial of skill, the whole concourse of people entreated him with one voice to restore Palfurius Sura to his place in the senate, from which he had been long before expelled–he having then carried away the prize of eloquence from all the orators who had contended for it,–he did not vouchsafe to give them any answer, but only commanded silence to be proclaimed by the voice of the crier. With equal arrogance, when he dictated the form of a letter to be used by his procurators, he began it thus: "Our lord and god commands so and so;" whence it became a rule that no one should style him otherwise either in writing or speaking. He suffered no statues to be erected for him in the Capitol, unless they were of gold and silver, and of a certain weight. He erected so many magnificent gates and arches, surmounted by representations of chariots drawn by four horses, and other triumphal ornaments, in different quarters of the city, that a wag inscribed on one of the arches the Greek word Axkei, "It is enough."[189] He filled the office of consul seventeen times, which no one had ever done before him, and for the seven middle occasions in successive years; but in scarcely any of them had he more than the title; for he never continued in office beyond the calends of May [the 1st May], and for the most part only till the ides of January [13th January]. After his two triumphs, when he assumed the cognomen of Germanicus, he called the months of September and October, Germanicus and Domitian, after his own names, because he commenced his reign in the one, and was born in the other.

XIV. Becoming by these means universally

---

189   The pun turns on the similar sound of the Greek word for "enough," and the Latin word for "an arch."

Titus Flavius Domitianus

feared and odious, he was at last taken off by a conspiracy of his friends and favourite freedmen, in concert with his wife[190]. He had long entertained a suspicion of the year and day when he should die, and even of the very hour and manner of his death; all which he had learned from the Chaldaeans, when he was a very young man. His father once at supper laughed at him for refusing to eat some mushrooms, saying, that if he knew his fate, he would rather be afraid of the sword. Being, therefore, in perpetual apprehension and anxiety, he was keenly alive to the slightest suspicions, insomuch that he is thought to have withdrawn the edict ordering the destruction of the vines, chiefly because the copies of it which were dispersed had the following lines written upon them:

Kaen me phagaes epi rizanomos epi

---

190   Domitia, who had been repudiated for an intrigue with Paris, the actor, and afterwards taken back.

kartophoraeso,
Osson epispeisai Kaisari thuomeno.[191]
Gnaw thou my root, yet shall my juice suffice
To pour on Caesar's head in sacrifice.

It was from the same principle of fear, that he refused a new honour, devised and offered him by the senate, though he was greedy of all such compliments. It was this: "that as often as he held the consulship, Roman knights, chosen by lot, should walk before him, clad in the Trabea, with lances in their hands, amongst his lictors and apparitors." As the time of the

---

191   The lines, with a slight accommodation, are borrowed from the poet Evenus, Anthol. i. vi. i., who applies them to a goat, the great enemy of vineyards. Ovid, Fasti, i. 357, thus paraphrases them:
Rode caper vitem, tamen hinc, cum staris ad aram,
In tua quod spargi cornua possit erit.

danger which he apprehended drew near, he became daily more and more disturbed in mind; insomuch that he lined the walls of the porticos in which he used to walk, with the stone called Phengites[192], by the reflection of which he could see every object behind him. He seldom gave an audience to persons in custody, unless in private, being alone, and he himself holding their chains in his hand. To convince his domestics that the life of a master was not to be attempted upon any pretext, however plausible, he condemned to death Epaphroditus his secretary, because it was believed that he had assisted Nero, in his extremity, to kill himself.

XV. His last victim was Flavius Clemens[193], his cousin-german, a man below contempt

---

192   Pliny describes this stone as being brought from Cappadocia, and says that it was as hard as marble, white and translucent, cxxiv. c. 22.

193   See note to c. xvii.

for his want of energy, whose sons, then of very tender age, he had avowedly destined for his successors, and, discarding their former names, had ordered one to be called Vespasian, and the other Domitian. Nevertheless, he suddenly put him to death upon some very slight suspicion[194], almost before he was well out of his consulship. By this violent act the very much hastened his own destruction. During eight months together there was so much lightning at Rome, and such accounts of the phaenomenon were brought from other parts, that at last he cried out, "Let him now strike whom he will." The Capitol was struck by lightning, as well as the temple of the Flavian family, with the Palatine-house, and his own bed-chamber. The tablet also, inscribed upon the base of his triumphal statue was carried away by the violence of the storm, and fell upon a

---

194   The guilt imputed to them was atheism and Jewish (Christian?) manners. Dion, lxvii. 1112.

neighbouring monument. The tree which just before the advancement of Vespasian had been prostrated, and rose again[195], suddenly fell to the ground. The goddess Fortune of Praeneste, to whom it was his custom on new year's day to commend the empire for the ensuing year, and who had always given him a favourable reply, at last returned him a melancholy answer, not without mention of blood. He dreamt that Minerva, whom he worshipped even to a superstitious excess, was withdrawing from her sanctuary, declaring she could protect him no longer, because she was disarmed by Jupiter. Nothing, however, so much affected him as an answer given by Ascletario, the astrologer, and his subsequent fate. This person had been informed against, and did not deny his having predicted some future events, of which, from the principles of his art, he confessed he had a foreknowledge.

---

195   See VESPASIAN, c. v.

Domitian asked him, what end he thought he should come to himself? To which replying, "I shall in a short time be torn to pieces by dogs," he ordered him immediately to be slain, and, in order to demonstrate the vanity of his art, to be carefully buried. But during the preparations for executing this order, it happened that the funeral pile was blown down by a sudden storm, and the body, half-burnt, was torn to pieces by dogs; which being observed by Latinus, the comic actor, as he chanced to pass that way, he told it, amongst the other news of the day, to the emperor at supper.

XVI. The day before his death, he ordered some dates[196], served up at table, to be

---

196   Columella (R. R. xi. 2.) enumerates dates among the foreign fruits cultivated in Italy, cherries, dates, apricots, and almonds; and Pliny, xv. 14, informs us that Sextus Papinius was the first who introduced the date tree, having brought it from Africa, in the latter days of Augustus.

kept till the next day, adding, "If I have the luck to use them." And turning to those who were nearest him, he said, "To-morrow the moon in Aquarius will be bloody instead of watery, and an event will happen, which will be much talked of all the world over." About midnight, he was so terrified that he leaped out of bed. That morning he tried and passed sentence on a soothsayer sent from Germany, who being consulted about the lightning that had lately happened, predicted from it a change of government. The blood running down his face as he scratched an ulcerous tumour on his forehead, he said, "Would this were all that is to befall me!" Then, upon his asking the time of the day, instead of five o'clock, which was the hour he dreaded, they purposely told him it was six. Overjoyed at this information; as if all danger were now passed, and hastening to the bath, Parthenius, his chamberlain, stopped him, by saying that there was a person come to wait upon him about a matter of great importance, which would admit of no delay. Upon this, ordering all persons to withdraw, he retired into his chamber, and was there slain.

XVII. Concerning the contrivance and mode of his death, the common account is this. The conspirators being in some doubt when and where they should attack him, whether while he was in the bath, or at supper, Stephanus, a steward of Domitilla's[197], then under prosecution for defrauding his mistress, offered them his advice and assistance; and wrapping

---

197   Some suppose that Domitilla was the wife of Flavius Clemens (c. xv.), both of whom were condemned by Domitian for their "impiety," by which it is probably meant that they were suspected of favouring Christianity. Eusebius makes Flavia Domitilla the niece of Flavius Clemens, and says that she was banished to Ponza, for having become a Christian. Clemens Romanus, the second bishop of Rome, is said to have been of this family.

up his left arm, as if it was hurt, in wool and bandages for some days, to prevent suspicion, at the hour appointed, he secreted a dagger in them. Pretending then to make a discovery of a conspiracy, and being for that reason admitted, he presented to the emperor a memorial, and while he was reading it in great astonishment, stabbed him in the groin. But Domitian, though wounded, making resistance, Clodianus, one of his guards, Maximus, a freedman of Parthenius's, Saturius, his principal chamberlain, with some gladiators, fell upon him, and stabbed him in seven places. A boy who had the charge of the Lares in his bed-chamber, and was then in attendance as usual, gave these further particulars: that he was ordered by Domitian, upon receiving his first wound, to reach him a dagger which lay under his pillow, and call in his domestics; but that he found nothing at the head of the bed, excepting the hilt of a poniard, and that all the doors were fastened: that the emperor in the mean time got hold of Stephanus, and throwing him upon the ground, struggled a long time with him; one while endeavouring to wrench the dagger from him, another while, though his fingers were miserably mangled, to tear out his eyes. He was slain upon the fourteenth of the calends of October [18th Sept.], in the forty-fifth year of his age, and the fifteenth of his reign[198]. His corpse was carried out upon a common bier by the public bearers, and buried by his nurse Phyllis, at his suburban villa on the Latin Way. But she afterwards privately conveyed his remains to the temple of the Flavian family[199], and mingled them with the ashes of Julia, the daughter of Titus, whom she had also nursed.

XVIII. He was tall in stature, his face modest, and very ruddy; he had large eyes, but was dim-sighted; naturally graceful in his

---

198   A.U.C. 849.
199   See c. v.

person, particularly in his youth, excepting only that his toes were bent somewhat inward, he was at last disfigured by baldness, corpulence, and the slenderness of his legs, which were reduced by a long illness. He was so sensible how much the modesty of his countenance recommended him, that he once made this boast to the senate, "Thus far you have approved both of my disposition and my countenance." His baldness so much annoyed him, that he considered it an affront to himself, if any other person was reproached with it, either in jest or in earnest; though in a small tract he published, addressed to a friend, "concerning the preservation of the hair," he uses for their mutual consolation the words following:

Ouch oraas oios kago kalos te megas te;
Seest thou my graceful mien, my stately form?

"and yet the fate of my hair awaits me; however, I bear with fortitude this loss of my hair while I am still young. Remember that nothing is more fascinating than beauty, but nothing of shorter duration."

XIX. He so shrunk from undergoing fatigue, that he scarcely ever walked through the city on foot. In his expeditions and on a march, he seldom rode on horseback; but was generally carried in a litter. He had no inclination for the exercise of arms, but was very expert in the use of the bow. Many persons have seen him often kill a hundred wild animals, of various kinds, at his Alban retreat, and fix his arrows in their heads with such dexterity, that he could, in two shots, plant them, like a pair of horns, in each. He would sometimes direct his arrows against the hand of a boy standing at a distance, and expanded as a mark, with such precision, that they all passed between the boy's fingers, without hurting him.

XX. In the beginning of his reign, he gave up the study of the liberal sciences, though he took care to restore, at a vast expense, the libraries which had been burnt down; collecting manuscripts from all parts, and sending scribes to Alexandria[200], either to copy or correct them. Yet he never gave himself the trouble of reading history or poetry, or of employing his pen even for his private purposes. He perused nothing but the Commentaries and Acts of Tiberius Caesar. His letters, speeches, and edicts, were all drawn up for him by others;

---

200 The famous library of Alexandria collected by Ptolemy Philadelphus had been burnt by accident in the wars. But we find from this passage in Suetonius that part of it was saved, or fresh collections had been made. Seneca (de Tranquill. c. ix. 7) informs us that forty thousand volumes were burnt; and Gellius states that in his time the number of volumes amounted to nearly seventy thousand.

though he could converse with elegance, and sometimes expressed himself in memorable sentiments. "I could wish," said he once, "that I was but as handsome as Metius fancies himself to be." And of the head of some one whose hair was partly reddish, and partly grey, he said, "that it was snow sprinkled with mead."

XXI. "The lot of princes," he remarked, "was very miserable, for no one believed them when they discovered a conspiracy, until they were murdered." When he had leisure, he amused himself with dice, even on days that were not festivals, and in the morning. He went to the bath early, and made a plentiful dinner, insomuch that he seldom ate more at supper than a Matian apple[201], to which he added a draught of

---

201   This favourite apple, mentioned by Columella and Pliny, took its name from C. Matius, a Roman knight, and friend of Augustus, who first introduced it. Pliny tells us that Matius was also the first who brought into vogue the

wine, out of a small flask. He gave frequent and splendid entertainments, but they were soon over, for he never prolonged them after sun-set, and indulged in no revel after. For, till bed-time, he did nothing else but walk by himself in private.

XXII. He was insatiable in his lusts, calling frequent commerce with women, as if it was a sort of exercise, klinopalaen, bed-wrestling; and it was reported that he plucked the hair from his concubines, and swam about in company with the lowest prostitutes. His brother's daughter[202] was offered him in marriage when she was a virgin; but being at that time enamoured of Domitia, he obstinately refused her. Yet not long afterwards, when she was given to another, he was ready enough to debauch her, and that even while Titus was living. But after she had lost both her father and her husband, he loved her most passionately,

practice of clipping groves.
202   Julia, the daughter of Titus.

and without disguise; insomuch that he was the occasion of her death, by obliging her to procure a miscarriage when she was with child by him.

XXIII. The people shewed little concern at his death, but the soldiers were roused by it to great indignation, and immediately endeavoured to have him ranked among the gods. They were also ready to revenge his loss, if there had been any to take the lead. However, they soon after effected it, by resolutely demanding the punishment of all those who had been concerned in his assassination. On the other hand, the senate was so overjoyed, that they met in all haste, and in a full assembly reviled his memory in the most bitter terms; ordering ladders to be brought in, and his shields and images to be pulled down before their eyes, and dashed in pieces upon the floor of the senate-house passing at the same time a decree to obliterate his titles every where, and abolish all memory of him. A few months before he was slain, a raven on the Capitol uttered these words: "All will be well." Some person gave the following interpretation of this prodigy:

Nuper Tarpeio quae sedit culmine cornix.
"Est bene," non potuit dicere; dixit, "Erit."
Late croaked a raven from Tarpeia's height,
"All is not yet, but shall be, right."

They say likewise that Domitian dreamed that a golden hump grew out of the back of his neck, which he considered as a certain sign of happy days for the empire after him. Such an auspicious change indeed shortly afterwards took place, through the justice and moderation of the succeeding emperors.

* * * * * *

If we view Domitian in the different lights in which he is represented, during his lifetime and after his decease, his character and conduct discover a greater diversity than is commonly observed in the objects of historical detail. But as posthumous character is always the most just, its decisive verdict affords the surest criterion by which this variegated emperor must be estimated by impartial posterity. According to this rule, it is beyond a doubt that his vices were more predominant than his virtues: and when we follow him into his closet, for some time after his accession, when he was thirty years of age, the frivolity of his daily employment, in the killing of flies, exhibits an instance of dissipation, which surpasses all that has been recorded of his imperial predecessors. The encouragement, however, which the first Vespasian had shown to literature, continued to operate during the present reign; and we behold the first fruits of its auspicious influence in the valuable treatise of QUINTILIAN.

Of the life of this celebrated writer, little is known upon any authority that has a title to much credit. We learn, however, that he was the son of a lawyer in the service of some of the preceding emperors, and was born in Rome, though in what consulship, or under what emperor, it is impossible to determine. He married a woman of a noble family, by whom he had two sons. The mother died in the flower of her age, and the sons, at the distance of some time from each other, when their father was advanced in years. The precise time of Quintilian's own death is equally inauthenticated with that of his birth; nor can we rely upon an author of suspicious veracity, who says that he passed the latter part of his life in a state of indigence which was alleviated by the liberality of his pupil, Pliny the Younger. Quintilian opened a school of rhetoric at Rome, where he not only discharged that labourious employment with great applause, during more than twenty years, but pleaded at the bar, and was the first who obtained a salary from the state, for executing the office of a public teacher. He was also appointed by Domitian preceptor to the two young princes who were intended to succeed him on the throne.

After his retirement from the situation of a teacher, Quintilian devoted his attention to the study of literature, and composed a treatise on the Causes of the Corruption of Eloquence. At the earnest solicitation of his friends, he was afterwards induced to undertake his Institutiones Oratoriae, the most elaborate system of oratory extant in any language. This work is divided into twelve books, in which the author treats with great precision of the qualities of a perfect orator; explaining not only the fundamental principles of eloquence, as connected with the constitution of the human mind, but pointing out, both by argument and observation, the most successful method of exercising that admirable art, for the accomplishment of its purpose. So minutely, and upon so extensive a plan, has he prosecuted the subject, that he delineates the education suitable to a perfect orator, from the stage of infancy in the cradle, to the consummation of rhetorical fame, in the pursuits of the bar, or those, in general, of any public assembly. It is sufficient to say, that in the execution of this elaborate work, Quintilian has called to the assistance of his own acute and comprehensive understanding, the profound penetration of Aristotle, the exquisite graces of Cicero; all the stores of observation, experience, and practice; and in a word, the whole accumulated exertions of ancient genius on the subject of oratory.

It may justly be regarded as an extraordinary circumstance in the progress of scientific improvement, that the endowments of a perfect orator were never fully exhibited to the world, until it had become dangerous to exercise them for the important purposes for which they were originally cultivated. And it is no less remarkable, that, under all the violence and caprice of imperial despotism which the Romans had now experienced, their sensibility to the enjoyment of poetical compositions remained still unabated; as if it served to console the nation for the irretrievable loss of public liberty. From this source of entertainment, they reaped more pleasure during the present reign, than they had done since the time of Augustus. The poets of this period were Juvenal, Statius, and Martial.

JUVENAL was born at Aquinum, but in what year is uncertain; though, from some circumstances, it seems to have been in the reign of Augustus. Some say that he was the son of a freedman, while others, without specifying the condition of his father, relate only that he was brought up by a freedman. He came at an early age to Rome, where he declaimed for many years, and, pleaded causes in the forum with great applause; but at last he betook himself to the writing of satires, in which he acquired great fame. One of the first, and the most constant object of is satire, was the pantomime Paris, the great favourite of the emperor Nero, and afterwards of Domitian. During the reign of the former of these emperors, no resentment was shown towards the poet; but he experienced not the same impunity after the accession of the latter; when, to remove him from the capital, he was sent as governor to the frontiers of Egypt, but in reality, into an honourable exile. According to some authors, he died of chagrin in that province: but this is not authenticated, and seems to be a mistake: for in some of Martial's epigrams, which appear to have been written after the death of Domitian, Juvenal is spoken of as residing at Rome. It is said that he lived to upwards of eighty years of age.

The remaining compositions of this author are sixteen satires, all written against the dissipation and enormous vices which prevailed at Rome in his time. The various objects of animadversion are painted in the strongest colours, and placed in the most conspicuous points of view. Giving loose reins to just and moral indignation, Juvenal is every where animated, vehement, petulant, and incessantly acrimonious. Disdaining the more lenient modes of correction, or despairing of their success, he neither adopts the raillery of Horace, nor the derision of Persius, but prosecutes vice and folly with all the severity of sentiment, passion, and expression. He sometimes exhibits a mixture of humour with his invectives; but it is a humour which partakes more of virulent rage than of pleasantry; broad, hostile, but coarse, and rivalling in indelicacy the profligate manners which it assails. The satires of Juvenal abound in philosophical apophthegms; and, where they are not sullied by obscene description, are supported with a uniform air of virtuous elevation. Amidst all the intemperance of sarcasm, his numbers are harmonious. Had his zeal permitted him to direct the current of his impetuous genius into the channel of ridicule, and endeavour to put to shame the vices and follies of those licentious times, as much as he perhaps exasperated conviction rather than excited contrition, he would have carried satire to the highest possible pitch, both of literary excellence and moral utility. With every abatement of attainable perfection, we hesitate not to place him at the head of this arduous department of poetry.

Of STATIUS no farther particulars are preserved than that he was born at Naples; that his father's name was Statius of Epirus, and his mother's Agelina, and that he died about the end of the first century of the Christian era. Some have conjectured that he maintained himself by writing for the stage, but of this there is no sufficient evidence; and if ever he composed dramatic productions, they have perished. The works of Statius now extant, are two poems, viz. the Thebais and the Achilleis, besides a collection, named Silvae.

The Thebais consists of twelve books, and the subject of it is the Theban war, which happened 1236 years before the Christian era, in consequence of a dispute between Eteocles and Polynices, the sons of Oedipus and Jocasta. These brothers had entered into an agreement with each other to reign alternately for a year at a time; and Eteocles being the elder, got first possession of the throne. This prince refusing to abdicate at the expiration of the year, Polynices fled to Argos, where marrying Argia, the daughter of Adrastus, king of that country, he procured the assistance of his father-in-law, to enforce the engagement stipulated with his brother Eteocles. The Argives marched under the command of seven able generals, who were to attack separately the seven gates of Thebes. After much blood had been spilt without any effect, it was at last agreed between the two parties, that the brothers should determine the dispute by single combat. In the desperate engagement which ensued, they both fell; and being burnt together upon the funeral pile, it is said that their ashes separated, as if actuated by the implacable resentment which they had borne to each other.

If we except the Aeneid, this is the only Latin production extant which is epic in its form; and it likewise approaches nearest in merit to that celebrated poem, which Statius appears to have been ambitious of emulating. In unity and greatness of action, the Thebais corresponds to the laws of the Epopea; but the fable may be regarded as defective in some particulars, which, however, arise more from the nature of the subject, than from any fault of the poet. The distinction of the hero is not sufficiently prominent; and the poem possesses not those circumstances which are requisite towards interesting the reader's affections in the issue of the contest. To this it may be added, that the unnatural complexion of the incestuous progeny diffuses a kind of gloom which obscures the splendour of thought, and restrains the sympathetic indulgence of fancy to some of the boldest excursions of the poet. For grandeur, however, and animation of sentiment and description, as well as for harmony of numbers, the Thebais is eminently conspicuous, and deserves to be held in a much higher degree of estimation than it has generally obtained. In the contrivance of some of the episodes, and frequently in the modes of expression, Statius keeps an attentive eye to the style of Virgil. It is said that he was twelve years employed in the composition of this poem; and we have his own authority for affirming, that he polished it with all the care and assiduity practised by the poets in the Augustan age:

**Quippe, te fido monitore, nostra
Thebais, multa cruciata lima,
Tentat audaci fide Mantuanae
Gaudia famae.–Silvae, lib. iv. 7.**

**For, taught by you, with steadfast care
I trim my "Song of Thebes," and dare
With generous rivalry to share
The glories of the Mantuan bard.**

The Achilleis relates to the same hero who is celebrated by Homer in the Iliad; but it is the previous history of Achilles, not his conduct in the Trojan war, which forms the subject of the poem of Statius. While the young hero is under the care of the Centaur Chiron, Thetis makes a visit to the preceptor's sequestered habitation, where, to save her son from the fate which, it was predicted, would befall him at Troy, if he should go to the siege of that place, she orders him to be dressed in the disguise of a girl, and sent to live in the family of Lycomedes, king of Scyros. But as Troy could not be taken without the aid of Achilles, Ulysses, accompanied by Diomede, is deputed by the Greeks to go to Scyros, and bring him thence to the Grecian camp. The artifice by which the sagacious ambassador detected Achilles amongst his female companions, was by placing before them various articles of merchandise, amongst which was some armour. Achilles no sooner perceived the latter, than he eagerly seized a sword and shield, and manifesting the strongest emotions of heroic enthusiasm, discovered his sex. After an affectionate parting with Lycomedes' daughter, Deidamia, whom he left pregnant of a son, he set sail with the Grecian chiefs, and, during the voyage, gives them an account of the manner of his education with Chiron.

This poem consists of two books, in heroic measure, and is written with taste and fancy. Commentators are of opinion, that the Achilleis was left incomplete by the death of the author; but this is extremely improbable, from various circumstances, and appears to be founded only upon the word Hactenus, in the conclusion of the poem:

Hactenus annorum, comites, elementa meorum
Et memini, et meminisse juvat: scit caetera mater.
Thus far, companions dear, with mindful joy I've told
My youthful deeds; the rest my mother can unfold.

That any consequential reference was intended by hactenus, seems to me plainly contradicted by the words which immediately follow, scit caetera mater. Statius could not propose the giving any further account of Achilles's life, because a general narrative of it had been given in the first book. The voyage from Scyros to the Trojan coast, conducted with the celerity which suited the purpose of the poet, admitted of no incidents which required description or recital: and after the voyagers had reached the Grecian camp, it is reasonable to suppose, that the action of the Iliad immediately commenced. But that Statius had no design of extending the plan of the Achilleis beyond this period, is expressly declared in the exordium of the poem:

Magnanimum   Aeaciden, formidatamque
    Tonanti
Progeniem, et patrio vetitam succedere
    coelo,
Diva, refer; quanquam acta viri multum
    inclyta cantu
Maeonio; sed plura vacant. Nos ire per
    omnem
(Sic amor est) heroa velis, Scyroque
    latentem

Titus Flavius Domitianus

Dulichia proferre tuba: nec in Hectore
    tracto
Sistere, sed tota juvenem deducere
    Troja.
Aid me, O goddess! while I sing of him,
Who shook the Thunderer's throne,
    and, for his crime,
Was doomed to lose his birthright in
    the skies;
The great Aeacides. Maeonian strains
Have made his mighty deeds their
    glorious theme;
Still much remains: be mine the
    pleasing task
To trace the future hero's young career,
Not dragging Hector at his chariot
    wheels,
But while disguised in Scyros yet he
    lurked,
Till trumpet-stirred, he sprung to manly
    arms,
And sage Ulysses led him to the Trojan

coast.

The Silvae is a collection of poems almost entirely in heroic verse, divided into five books, and for the most part written extempore. Statius himself affirms, in his Dedication to Stella, that the production of none of them employed him more than two days; yet many of them consist of between one hundred and two hundred hexameter lines. We meet with one of two hundred and sixteen lines; one, of two hundred and thirty-four; one, of two hundred and sixty-two; and one of two hundred and seventy-seven; a rapidity of composition approaching to what Horace mentions of the poet Lucilius. It is no small encomium to observe, that, considered as extemporaneous productions, the meanest in the collection is far from meriting censure, either in point of sentiment or expression; and many of them contain passages which command our applause.

The poet MARTIAL, surnamed likewise

Coquus, was born at Bilbilis, in Spain, of obscure parents. At the age of twenty-one, he came to Rome, where he lived during five-and-thirty years under the emperors Galba, Otho, Vitellius, the two Vespasians, Domitian, Nerva, and the beginning of the reign of Trajan. He was the panegyrist of several of those emperors, by whom he was liberally rewarded, raised to the Equestrian order, and promoted by Domitian to the tribuneship; but being treated with coldness and neglect by Trajan, he returned to his native country, and, a few years after, ended his days, at the age of seventy-five.

He had lived at Rome in great splendour and affluence, as well as in high esteem for his poetical talents; but upon his return to Bilbilis, it is said that he experienced a great reverse of fortune, and was chiefly indebted for his support to the gratuitous benefactions of Pliny the Younger, whom he had extolled in some epigrams.

The poems of Martial consist of fourteen

books, all written in the epigrammatic form, to which species of composition, introduced by the Greeks, he had a peculiar propensity. Amidst such a multitude of verses, on a variety of subjects, often composed extempore, and many of them, probably, in the moments of fashionable dissipation, it is not surprising that we find a large number unworthy the genius of the author. Delicacy, and even decency, is often violated in the productions of Martial. Grasping at every thought which afforded even the shadow of ingenuity, he gave unlimited scope to the exercise of an active and fruitful imagination. In respect to composition, he is likewise liable to censure. At one time he wearies, and at another tantalises the reader, with the prolixity or ambiguity of his preambles. His prelusive sentiments are sometimes far-fetched, and converge not with a natural declination into the focus of epigram. In dispensing praise and censure, he often seems to be governed more by prejudice or policy, than by justice and truth; and he is more constantly attentive to the production of wit, than to the improvement of morality.

But while we remark the blemishes and imperfections of this poet, we must acknowledge his extraordinary merits. In composition he is, in general, elegant and correct; and where the subject is capable of connection with sentiment, his inventive ingenuity never fails to extract from it the essence of delight and surprise. His fancy is prolific of beautiful images, and his judgment expert in arranging them to the greatest advantage. He bestows panegyric with inimitable grace, and satirises with equal dexterity. In a fund of Attic salt, he surpasses every other writer; and though he seems to have at command all the varied stores of gall, he is not destitute of candour. With almost every kind of versification he appears to be familiar; and notwithstanding a facility of temper, too accommodating, perhaps, on many occasions, to the licentiousness of the times, we may venture from strong indications to pronounce, that, as a moralist, his principles were virtuous. It is observed of this author, by Pliny the Younger, that, though his compositions might, perhaps, not obtain immortality, he wrote as if they would. [Aeterna, quae scripsit, non erunt fortasse: ille tamen scripsit tanquam futura.] The character which Martial gives of his epigrams, is just and comprehensive:

Sunt bona, sunt quaedam mediocria, sunt mala plura,
Quae legis: hic aliter non fit, Avite, liber.

Some are good, some indifferent, and some again still worse;
Such, Avitus, you will find is a common case with verse.

THE END OF THE
TWELVE CAESARS

Lives of Eminent Grammarians

I. THE SCIENCE OF GRAMMAR[203] was in ancient times far from being in vogue at Rome; indeed, it was of little use in a rude state of society, when the people were engaged in constant wars, and had not much time to bestow on the cultivation of the

---

203 It will be understood that the terms Grammar and Grammarian have here a more extended sense than that which they convey in modern use. See the beginning of c. iv.

liberal arts[204]. At the outset, its pretensions were very slender, for the earliest men of learning, who were both poets and orators, may be considered as half-Greek:

---

204   Suetonius's account of the rude and unlettered state of society in the early times of Rome, is consistent with what we might infer, and with the accounts which have come down to us, of a community composed of the most daring and adventurous spirits thrown off by the neighbouring tribes, and whose sole occupations were rapine and war. But Cicero discovers the germs of mental cultivation among the Romans long before the period assigned to it by Suetonius, tracing them to the teaching of Pythagoras, who visited the Greek cities on the coast of Italy in the reign of Tarquinius Superbus.– Tusc. Quaest. iv. 1.

I speak of Livius[205] and Ennius[206], who are acknowledged to have taught both languages as well at Rome as in foreign parts[207]. But they only translated from the Greek, and if they composed anything of

---

205   Livius, whose cognomen Andronicus, intimates his extraction, was born of Greek parents. He began to teach at Rome in the consulship of Claudius Cento, the son of Appius Caecus, and Sempronius Tuditanus, A.U.C. 514. He must not be confounded with Titus Livius, the historian, who flourished in the Augustan age.

206   Ennius was a native of Calabria. He was born the year after the consulship mentioned in the preceding note, and lived to see at least his seventy-sixth year, for Gellius informs us that at that age he wrote the twelfth book of his Annals.

207   Porcius Cato found Ennius in Sardinia, when he conquered that island during his praetorship. He learnt Greek from Ennius there, and brought him to Rome on his return. Ennius taught Greek at Rome for a long course of years, having M. Cato among his pupils.

their own in Latin, it was only from what they had before read. For although there are those who say that this Ennius published two books, one on "Letters and Syllables," and the other on "Metres," Lucius Cotta has satisfactorily proved that they are not the works of the poet Ennius, but of another writer of the same name, to whom also the treatise on the "Rules of Augury" is attributed.

II. Crates of Mallos[208], then, was, in our opinion, the first who introduced the study of grammar at Rome. He was cotemporary with Aristarchus[209], and having been sent by king Attalus as envoy to the senate in the interval between the second and third Punic

---

208   Mallos was near Tarsus, in Cilicia. Crates was the son of Timocrates, a Stoic philosopher, who for his critical skill had the surname of Homericus.

209   Aristarchus flourished at Alexandria, in the reign of Ptolemy Philometer, whose son he educated.

wars[210], soon after the death of Ennius[211], he had the misfortune to fall into an open sewer in the Palatine quarter of the city, and broke his leg. After which, during the whole period of his embassy and convalescence, he gave frequent lectures, taking much pains to instruct his hearers, and he has left us an example well worthy of imitation. It was so far followed, that poems hitherto little known, the works either of deceased friends or other approved writers, were brought to light, and being read and commented on, were explained to others. Thus, Caius Octavius Lampadio edited the Punic War of Naevius[212], which having been written in one volume without

---

210   A.U.C. 535-602 or 605.
211   Cicero (De Clar. Orat. c. xx., De Senect. c. v. 1) places the death of Ennius A.U.C. 584, for which there are other authorities; but this differs from the account given in a former note.
212   The History of the first Punic War by Naevius is mentioned by Cicero, De Senect, c. 14.

any break in the manuscript, he divided into seven books. After that, Quintus Vargonteius undertook the Annals of Ennius, which he read on certain fixed days to crowded audiences. So Laelius Archelaus, and Vectius Philocomus, read and commented on the Satires of their friend Lucilius[213], which Lenaeus Pompeius, a freedman, tells us he studied under Archelaus; and Valerius Cato, under Philocomus. Two others also taught and promoted grammar in various branches, namely, Lucius Aelius Lanuvinus, the son-in-law of Quintus Aelius, and Servius Claudius, both of whom were Roman knights, and men who rendered great services both to learning and the republic.

III. Lucius Aelius had a double cognomen, for he was called Praeconius, because his father was a herald; Stilo, because he was in the habit of composing orations for most of the speakers of highest rank; indeed, he was

---

213   Lucilius, the poet, was born about A.U.C. 605.

so strong a partisan of the nobles, that he accompanied Quintus Metellus Numidicus[214] in his exile. Servius[215] having clandestinely obtained his father-in-law's book before it was published, was disowned for the fraud, which he took so much to heart, that, overwhelmed with shame and distress, he retired from Rome; and being seized with a fit of the gout, in his impatience, he applied a poisonous ointment to his feet, which half-killed him, so that his lower limbs mortified while he was still alive. After this, more attention was paid to the science of letters, and it grew in public estimation, insomuch, that men of the

---

214   Q. Metellus obtained the surname of Numidicus, on his triumph over Jugurtha, A.U.C. 644. Aelius, who was Varro's tutor, accompanied him to Rhodes or Smyrna, when he was unjustly banished, A.U.C. 653.
215   Servius Claudius (also called Clodius) is commended by Cicero, Fam. Epist. ix. 16, and his singular death mentioned by Pliny, xxv. 4.

highest rank did not hesitate in undertaking to write something on the subject; and it is related that sometimes there were no less than twenty celebrated scholars in Rome. So high was the value, and so great were the rewards, of grammarians, that Lutatius Daphnides, jocularly called "Pan's herd"[216] by Lenaeus Melissus, was purchased by Quintus Catullus for two hundred thousand sesterces, and shortly afterwards made a freedman; and that Lucius Apuleius, who was taken into the pay of Epicius Calvinus, a wealthy Roman knight, at the annual salary of ten thousand crowns, had many scholars. Grammar also penetrated into the provinces,

---

216   Daphnis, a shepherd, the son of Mercury, was said to have been brought up by Pan. The humorous turn given by Lenaeus to Lutatius's cognomen is not very clear. Daphnides is the plural of Daphnis; therefore the herd or company, agaema; and Pan was the god of rustics, and the inventor of the rude music of the reed.

and some of the most eminent amongst the learned taught it in foreign parts, particularly in Gallia Togata. In the number of these, we may reckon Octavius Teucer, Siscennius Jacchus, and Oppius Cares[217], who persisted in teaching to a most advanced period of his life, at a time when he was not only unable to walk, but his sight failed.

IV. The appellation of grammarian was borrowed from the Greeks; but at first, the Latins called such persons literati. Cornelius Nepos, also, in his book, where he draws a distinction between a literate and a philologist, says that in common phrase, those are properly called literati who are skilled in speaking or writing with care or accuracy, and those more especially deserve the name who translated the poets, and were called grammarians by the Greeks. It appears that they were named literators by Messala Corvinus, in one of his letters, when he says, "that it does not refer

---

217   Oppius Cares is said by Macrobius to have written a book on Forest Trees.

to Furius Bibaculus, nor even to Sigida, nor to Cato, the literator,"[218] meaning, doubtless, that Valerius Cato was both a poet and an eminent grammarian. Some there are who draw a distinction between a literati and a literator, as the Greeks do between a grammarian and a grammatist, applying the former term to men of real erudition, the latter to those whose pretensions to learning are moderate; and this opinion Orbilius supports by examples. For he says that in old times, when a company of slaves was offered for sale by any person, it was not customary, without good reason, to describe either of them in the catalogue as a literati, but only

---

218   Quintilian enumerates Bibaculus among the Roman poets in the same line with Catullus and Horace, Institut. x. 1. Of Sigida we know nothing; even the name is supposed to be incorrectly given. Apuleius mentions a Ticida, who is also noticed by Suetonius hereafter in c. xi., where likewise he gives an account of Valerius Cato.

as a literator, meaning that he was not a proficient in letters, but had a smattering of knowledge.

The early grammarians taught rhetoric also, and we have many of their treatises which include both sciences; whence it arose, I think, that in later times, although the two professions had then become distinct, the old custom was retained, or the grammarians introduced into their teaching some of the elements required for public speaking, such as the problem, the periphrasis, the choice of words, description of character, and the like; in order that they might not transfer their pupils to the rhetoricians no better than ill-taught boys. But I perceive that these lessons are now given up in some cases, on account of the want of application, or the tender years, of the scholar, for I do not believe that it arises from any dislike in the master. I recollect that when I was a boy it was the custom of one of these, whose name was Princeps, to take alternate days for declaiming and disputing; and sometimes he would lecture in the morning, and declaim in the afternoon, when he had his pulpit removed. I heard, also, that even within the memories of our own fathers, some of the pupils of the grammarians passed directly from the schools to the courts, and at once took a high place in the ranks of the most distinguished advocates. The professors at that time were, indeed, men of great eminence, of some of whom I may be able to give an account in the following chapters.

V. SAEVIUS[219] NICANOR first acquired fame and reputation by his teaching: and, besides, he made commentaries, the greater part of which, however, are said

---

219   Probably Suevius, of whom Macrobius informs us that he was the learned author of an Idyll, which had the title of the Mulberry Grove; observing, that "the peach which Suevius reckons as a species of the nuts, rather belongs to the tribe of apples."

to have been borrowed. He also wrote a satire, in which he informs us that he was a freedman, and had a double cognomen, in the following verses;

Saevius Nicanor Marci libertus negabit,
Saevius Posthumius idem, sed Marcus,
docebit.

What Saevius Nicanor, the freedman of
Marcus, will deny,
The same Saevius, called also
Posthumius Marcus, will assert.

It is reported, that in consequence of some infamy attached to his character, he retired to Sardinia, and there ended his days.

VI. AURELIUS OPILIUS[220], the freedman

---

220 Aurelius Opilius is mentioned by Symmachus and Gellius. His cotemporary and friend, Rutilius Rufus, having been a military tribune under Scipio in the Numantine war, wrote a history of it. He was consul A.U.C. 648,

of some Epicurean, first taught philosophy, then rhetoric, and last of all, grammar. Having closed his school, he followed Rutilius Rufus, when he was banished to Asia, and there the two friends grew old together. He also wrote several volumes on a variety of learned topics, nine books of which he distinguished by the number and names of the nine Muses; as he says, not without reason, they being the patrons of authors and poets. I observe that its title is given in several indexes by a single letter, but he uses two in the heading of a book called Pinax.

VII. MARCUS ANTONIUS GNIPHO[221], a free-born native of Gaul, was exposed in his infancy, and afterwards received his freedom from his foster-father; and, as some say, was

---

and unjustly banished, to the general grief of the people, A.U.C. 659.

221   Quintilian mentions Gnipho, Instit. i. 6. We find that Cicero was among his pupils. The date of his praetorship, given below, fixes the time when Gnipho flourished.

educated at Alexandria, where Dionysius Scytobrachion[222] was his fellow pupil. This, however, I am not very ready to believe, as the times at which they flourished scarcely agree. He is said to have been a man of great genius, of singular memory, well read in Greek as well as Latin, and of a most obliging and agreeable temper, who never haggled about remuneration, but generally left it to the liberality of his scholars. He first taught in the house of Julius Caesar[223], when the latter was yet but a boy, and, afterwards, in his own private house. He gave instruction in rhetoric also, teaching the rules of eloquence every day, but declaiming only on festivals. It is said that some very celebrated men frequented his school,–and, among others, Marcus Cicero,

---

222   This strange cognomen is supposed to have been derived from a cork arm, which supplied the place of one Dionysius had lost. He was a poet of Mitylene.
223   See before, JULIUS, c. xlvi.

during the time he held the praetorship[224]. He wrote a number of works, although he did not live beyond his fiftieth year; but Atteius, the philologist[225], says, that he left only two volumes, "De Latino Sermone;" and, that the other works ascribed to him, were composed by his disciples, and were not his, although his name is sometimes to be found in them.

VIII. M. POMPILIUS ANDRONICUS, a native of Syria, while he professed to be a grammarian, was considered an idle follower of the Epicurean sect, and little qualified to be a master of a school. Finding, therefore, that, at Rome, not only Antonius Gnipho, but even other teachers of less note were preferred to him, he retired to Cumae, where he lived at his ease; and, though he wrote several books, he was so needy, and reduced to such straits, as to be compelled to sell that excellent little work of his, "The Index to the Annals," for sixteen thousand

---

224   A.U.C. 687.
225   Suetonius gives his life in c. x.

sesterces. Orbilius has informed us, that he redeemed this work from the oblivion into which it had fallen, and took care to have it published with the author's name.

IX. ORBILIUS PUPILLUS, of Beneventum, being left an orphan, by the death of his parents, who both fell a sacrifice to the plots of their enemies on the same day, acted, at first, as apparitor to the magistrates. He then joined the troops in Macedonia, when he was first decorated with the plumed helmet[226], and, afterwards, promoted to serve on horseback. Having completed his military service, he resumed his studies, which he had pursued with no small diligence from his youth upwards; and, having been a professor for a long period in his own country, at last, during the consulship of Cicero, made his way to Rome, where he taught with more reputation than profit. For in one of his works he says, that "he was

---

226   A grade of inferior officers in the Roman armies, of which we have no very exact idea.

then very old, and lived in a garret." He also published a book with the title of Perialogos; containing complaints of the injurious treatment to which professors submitted, without seeking redress at the hands of parents. His sour temper betrayed itself, not only in his disputes with the sophists opposed to him, whom he lashed on every occasion, but also towards his scholars, as Horace tells us, who calls him "a flogger;"[227] and Domitius Marsus[228], who says of him:

Si quos Orbilius ferula scuticaque cecidit.
If those Orbilius with rod or ferule

---

227   Horace speaks feelingly on the subject: Memini quae plagosum mihi parvo Orbilium tractare. Epist. xi. i. 70.

I remember well when I was young, How old Orbilius thwacked me at my tasks.
228   Domitius Marsus wrote epigrams. He is mentioned by Ovid and Martial.

thrashed.

And not even men of rank escaped his sarcasms; for, before he became noticed, happening to be examined as a witness in a crowded court, Varro, the advocate on the other side, put the question to him, "What he did and by what profession he gained his livelihood?" He replied, "That he lived by removing hunchbacks from the sunshine into the shade," alluding to Muraena's deformity. He lived till he was near a hundred years old; but he had long lost his memory, as the verse of Bibaculus informs us:

**Orbilius ubinam est, literarum oblivio?
Where is Orbilius now, that wreck of
learning lost?**

His statue is shown in the Capitol at Beneventum. It stands on the left hand, and is sculptured in marble[229], representing him in a sitting posture, wearing the pallium, with two writing-cases in his hand. He left a son, named also Orbilius, who, like his father, was a professor of grammar.

X. ATTEIUS, THE PHILOLOGIST, a freedman, was born at Athens. Of him, Capito Atteius[230], the well-known jurisconsult, says that he was a rhetorician among the grammarians, and a grammarian among the rhetoricians. Asinius Pollio[231], in the book in which he finds fault with the writings of Sallust for his great affectation of obsolete

---

229   This is not the only instance mentioned by Suetonius of statues erected to learned men in the place of their birth or celebrity. Orbilius, as a schoolmaster, was represented in a sitting posture, and with the gown of the Greek philosophers.

230   Tacitus (Annal. cxi. 75) gives the character of Atteius Capito. He was consul A.U.C. 758.

231   Asinius Pollio; see JULIUS, c. xxx.

words, speaks thus: "In this work his chief assistant was a certain Atteius, a man of rank, a splendid Latin grammarian, the aider and preceptor of those who studied the practice of declamation; in short, one who claimed for himself the cognomen of Philologus." Writing to Lucius Hermas, he says, "that he had made great proficiency in Greek literature, and some in Latin; that he had been a hearer of Antonius Gnipho, and his Hermas[232], and afterwards began to teach others. Moreover, that he had for pupils many illustrious youths, among whom were the two brothers, Appius and Pulcher Claudius; and that he even accompanied them to their province." He appears to have assumed the name of Philologus, because, like Eratosthenes[233], who first adopted that

---

232   Whether Hermas was the son or scholar of Gnipho, does not appear,
233   Eratosthenes, an Athenian philosopher, flourished in Egypt, under three of the Ptolemies successively. Strabo often mentions him. See

cognomen, he was in high repute for his rich and varied stores of learning; which, indeed, is evident from his commentaries, though but few of them are extant. Another letter, however, to the same Hermas, shews that they were very numerous: "Remember," it says, "to recommend generally our Extracts, which we have collected, as you know, of all kinds, into eight hundred books." He afterwards formed an intimate acquaintance with Caius Sallustius, and, on his death, with Asinius Pollio; and when they undertook to write a history, he supplied the one with short annals of all Roman affairs, from which he could select at pleasure; and the other, with rules on the art of composition. I am, therefore, surprised that Asinius Pollio should have supposed that he was in the habit of collecting old words and figures of speech for Sallust, when he must have known that his own advice was,

---

xvii. p. 576.

that none but well known, and common and appropriate expressions should be made use of; and that, above all things, the obscurity of the style of Sallust, and his bold freedom in translations, should be avoided.

XI. VALERIUS CATO was, as some have informed us, the freedman of one Bursenus, a native of Gaul. He himself tells us, in his little work called "Indignatio," that he was born free, and being left an orphan, was exposed to be easily stripped of his patrimony during the licence of Sylla's administrations. He had a great number of distinguished pupils, and was highly esteemed as a preceptor suited to those who had a poetical turn, as appears from these short lines:

Cato grammaticus, Latina Siren,
Qui solus legit ac facit poetas.
Cato, the Latin Siren, grammar taught
and verse,
To form the poet skilled, and poetry
rehearse.

Besides his Treatise on Grammar, he composed some poems, of which, his Lydia and Diana are most admired. Ticida mentions his "Lydia."

Lydia, doctorum maxima cura liber.
"Lydia," a work to men of learning dear.

Cinna[234] thus notices the "Diana."

Secula permaneat nostri Diana Catonis.
Immortal be our Cato's song of Dian.

He lived to extreme old age, but in the lowest state of penury, and almost in actual want; having retired to a small cottage when he gave up his Tusculan villa to his creditors; as Bibaculus tells us:

---

234 Cornelius Helvius Cinna was an epigrammatic poet, of the same age as Catullus. Ovid mentions him, Tristia, xi. 435.

Si quis forte mei domum Catonis,
Depictas minio assulas, et illos
Custodis vidit hortulos Priapi,
Miratur, quibus ille disciplinis,
Tantam sit sapientiam assecutus,
Quam tres cauliculi et selibra farris;
Racemi duo, tegula sub una,
Ad summam prope nutriant senectam.

"If, perchance, any one has seen the house of my Cato, with marble slabs of the richest hues, and his gardens worthy of having Priapus[235] for their guardian, he may well wonder by what philosophy he has gained so much wisdom, that a daily allowance of three coleworts, half-a-pound of meal, and two bunches of grapes, under a narrow roof, should serve for his subsistence to extreme old age."

And he says in another place:

---

235   Priapus was worshipped as the protector of gardens.

Catonis modo, Galle, Tusculanum
Tota creditor urbe venditahat.
Mirati sumus unicum magistrum,
Summum grammaticum, optimum
    poetam,
Omnes solvere posse quaestiones,
Unum difficile expedire nomen.
En cor Zenodoti, en jecur Cratetis!

"We lately saw, my Gallus, Cato's Tusculan villa exposed to public sale by his creditors; and wondered that such an unrivalled master of the schools, most eminent grammarian, and accomplished poet, could solve all propositions and yet found one question too difficult for him to settle,–how to pay his debts. We find in him the genius of Zenodotus[236], the wisdom of Crates."[237]

---

236   Zenodotus, the grammarian, was librarian to the first Ptolemy at Alexandria, and tutor to his sons.

237   For Crates, see before, p. 507.

XII. CORNELIUS EPICADIUS, a freedman of Lucius Cornelius Sylla, the dictator, was his apparitor in the Augural priesthood, and much beloved by his son Faustus; so that he was proud to call himself the freedman of both. He completed the last book of Sylla's Commentaries, which his patron had left unfinished.[238]

XIII. LABERIUS HIERA was bought by his master out of a slave-dealer's cage, and obtained his freedom on account of his devotion to learning. It is reported that his disinterestedness was such, that he gave gratuitous instruction to the children of those who were proscribed in the time

---

238   We find from Plutarch that Sylla was employed two days before his death, in completing the twenty-second book of his Commentaries; and, foreseeing his fate, entrusted them to the care of Lucullus, who, with the assistance of Epicadius, corrected and arranged them. Epicadius also wrote on Heroic verse, and Cognomina.

of Sylla.

XIV. CURTIUS NICIA was the intimate friend of Cneius Pompeius and Caius Memmius; but having carried notes from Memmius to Pompey's wife[239], when she was debauched by Memmius, Pompey was indignant, and forbad him his house. He was also on familiar terms with Marcus Cicero, who thus speaks of him in his epistle to Dolabella[240]: "I have more need of receiving letters from you, than you have of desiring them from me. For there is nothing going on at Rome in which I think you would take any interest, except, perhaps, that you may like to know that I am appointed umpire between our friends Nicias and Vidius. The one, it appears, alleges in two short verses that Nicias owes him money; the other, like an Aristarchus, cavils at them. I, like an old

239   Plutarch, in his Life of Caesar, speaks of the loose conduct of Mucia, Pompey's wife, during her husband's absence.
240   Fam. Epist. 9.

critic, am to decide whether they are Nicias's or spurious."

Again, in a letter to Atticus[241], he says: "As to what you write about Nicias, nothing could give me greater pleasure than to have him with me, if I was in a position to enjoy his society; but my province is to me a place of retirement and solitude. Sicca easily reconciled himself to this state of things, and, therefore, I would prefer having him. Besides, you are well aware of the feebleness, and the nice and luxurious habits, of our friend Nicias. Why should I be the means of making him uncomfortable, when he can afford me no pleasure? At the same time, I value his goodwill."

XV. LENAEUS was a freedman of Pompey the Great, and attended him in most of his expeditions. On the death of his patron and his sons, he supported himself by teaching in a school which he opened

---

241   Cicero ad Att. xii. 36.

near the temple of Tellus, in the Carium, in the quarter of the city where the house of the Pompeys stood[242]. Such was his regard for his patron's memory, that when Sallust described him as having a brazen face, and a shameless mind, he lashed the historian in a most bitter satire[243], as "a bull's-pizzle, a gormandizer, a braggart, and a tippler, a man whose life and writings were equally monstrous;" besides charging him with being "a most unskilful plagiarist, who borrowed the language of Cato and other old writers." It is related, that, in his youth, having escaped from slavery by the contrivance of some of his friends, he

---

242   See before, AUGUSTUS, c. v.

243   Lenaeus was not singular in his censure of Sallust. Lactantius, 11. 12, gives him an infamous character; and Horace says of him,
Libertinarum dico;
Sallustius in quas
Non minus insanit; quam qui moechatur.–Sat. i. 2. 48.

took refuge in his own country; and, that after he had applied himself to the liberal arts, he brought the price of his freedom to his former master, who, however, struck by his talents and learning, gave him manumission gratuitously.

XVI. QUINTUS CAECILIUS, an Epirot by descent, but born at Tusculum, was a freedman of Atticus Satrius, a Roman knight, to whom Cicero addressed his Epistles[244]. He became the tutor of his patron's daughter[245],

---

244   The name of the well known Roman knight, to whom Cicero addressed his Epistles, was Titus Pomponius Atticus. Although Satrius was the name of a family at Rome, no connection between it and Atticus can be found, so that the text is supposed to be corrupt. Quintus Caecilius was an uncle of Atticus, and adopted him. The freedman mentioned in this chapter probably assumed his name, he having been the property of Caecilius; as it was the custom for freedmen to adopt the names of their patrons.

245   Suetonius, TIBERIUS, c. viii. Her name

who was contracted to Marcus Agrippa, but being suspected of an illicit intercourse with her, and sent away on that account, he betook himself to Cornelius Gallus, and lived with him on terms of the greatest intimacy, which, indeed, was imputed to Gallus as one of his heaviest offences, by Augustus. Then, after the condemnation and death of Gallus[246], he opened a school, but had few pupils, and those very young, nor any belonging to the higher orders, excepting the children of those he could not refuse to admit. He was the first, it is said, who held disputations in Latin, and who began to lecture on Virgil and the other modern poets; which the verse of Domitius Marcus[247] points out.

Epirota tenellorum nutricula vatum.
The Epirot who,
With tender care, our unfledged poets

was Pomponia.
246   See AUGUSTUS, c. lxvi.
247   He is mentioned before, c. ix.

nursed.

XVII. VERRIUS FLACCUS[248], a freedman, distinguished himself by a new mode of teaching; for it was his practice to exercise the wits of his scholars, by encouraging emulation among them; not only proposing the subjects on which they were to write, but offering rewards for those who were successful in the contest. These consisted of some ancient, handsome, or rare book. Being, in consequence, selected by Augustus, as preceptor to his grandsons, he transferred his entire school to the Palatium, but with the understanding that he should admit no fresh scholars. The hall in Catiline's house, which had then been added to the palace, was assigned him for his school,

---

248   Verrius Flaccus is mentioned by St. Jerome, in conjunction with Athenodorus of Tarsus, a Stoic philosopher, to have flourished A.M.C. 2024, which is A.U.C. 759; A.D. 9. He is also praised by Gellius, Macrobius, Pliny, and Priscian.

with a yearly allowance of one hundred thousand sesterces. He died of old age, in the reign of Tiberius. There is a statue of him at Praeneste, in the semi-circle at the lower side of the forum, where he had set up calendars arranged by himself, and inscribed on slabs of marble.

XVIII. LUCIUS CRASSITIUS, a native of Tarentum, and in rank a freedman, had the cognomen of Pasides, which he afterwards changed for Pansa. His first employment was connected with the stage, and his business was to assist the writers of farces. After that, he took to giving lessons in a gallery attached to a house, until his commentary on "The Smyrna"[249] so brought him into notice, that the following lines were written on him:

Uni Crassitio se credere Smyrna

---

249   Cinna wrote a poem, which he called "Smyrna," and was nine years in composing, as Catullus informs us, 93. 1.

probavit.
Desinite indocti, conjugio hanc petere.
Soli Crassitio se dixit nubere velle:
Intima cui soli nota sua exstiterint.

Crassitius only counts on Smyrna's
  love,
Fruitless the wooings of the unlettered
  prove;
Crassitius she receives with loving
  arms,
For he alone unveiled her hidden
  charms.

However, after having taught many scholars, some of whom were of high rank, and amongst others, Julius Antonius, the triumvir's son, so that he might be even compared with Verrius Flaccus; he suddenly closed his school, and joined the sect of Quintus Septimius, the philosopher.

XIX. SCRIBONIUS APHRODISIUS, the

slave and disciple of Orbilius, who was afterwards redeemed and presented with his freedom by Scribonia[250], the daughter of Libo who had been the wife of Augustus, taught in the time of Verrius; whose books on Orthography he also revised, not without some severe remarks on his pursuits and conduct.

XX. C. JULIUS HYGINUS, a freedman of Augustus, was a native of Spain, (although some say he was born at Alexandria,) and that when that city was taken, Caesar brought him, then a boy, to Rome. He closely and carefully imitated Cornelius Alexander[251], a

---

250   See AUGUSTUS, cc. lxii. lxix.

251   Cornelius Alexander, who had also the name of Polyhistor, was born at Miletus, and being taken prisoner, and bought by Cornelius, was brought to Rome, and becoming his teacher, had his freedom given him, with the name of his patron. He flourished in the time of Sylla, and composed a great number of works; amongst which were five books on Rome.

Greek grammarian, who, for his antiquarian knowledge, was called by many Polyhistor, and by some History. He had the charge of the Palatine library, but that did not prevent him from having many scholars; and he was one of the most intimate friends of the poet Ovid, and of Caius Licinius, the historian, a man of consular rank[252], who has related that Hyginus died very poor, and was supported by his liberality as long as he lived. Julius Modestus[253], who was a freedman of Hyginus, followed the footsteps

---

Suetonius has already told us (AUGUSTUS, xxix.) that he had the care of the Palatine Library.

252   No such consul as Caius Licinius appears in the Fasti; and it is supposed to be a mistake for C. Atinius, who was the colleague of Cn. Domitius Calvinus, A.U.C. 713, and wrote a book on the Civil War.

253   Julius Modestus, in whom the name of the Julian family was still preserved, is mentioned with approbation by Gellius, Martial, Quintilian, and others.

of his patron in his studies and learning.

XXI. CAIUS MELISSUS[254], a native of Spoletum, was free-born, but having been exposed by his parents in consequence of quarrels between them, he received a good education from his foster-father, by whose care and industry he was brought up, and was made a present of to Mecaenas, as a grammarian. Finding himself valued and treated as a friend, he preferred to continue in his state of servitude, although he was claimed by his mother, choosing rather his present condition than that which his real origin entitled him to. In consequence, his freedom was speedily given him, and he even became a favourite with Augustus. By his appointment he was made curator of the library in the portico of Octavia[255]; and, as he himself informs us, undertook to compose, when he was a sexagenarian,

---

254   Melissus is mentioned by Ovid, De Pontif. iv 16-30.

255   See AUGUSTUS, c. xxix. p. 93, and note.

his books of "Witticisms," which are now called "The Book of Jests." Of these he accomplished one hundred and fifty, to which he afterwards added several more. He also composed a new kind of story about those who wore the toga, and called it "Trabeat."[256]

XXII. MARCUS POMPONIUS MARCELLUS, a very severe critic of the Latin tongue, who sometimes pleaded causes, in a certain address on the plaintiff's behalf, persisted in charging his adversary with making a solecism, until Cassius Severus appealed to the judges to grant an adjournment until his client should produce another grammarian, as he was not prepared to enter into a controversy respecting a solecism, instead of defending his client's rights. On another occasion, when he had found fault with

---

256 The trabea was a white robe, with a purple border, of a different fashion from the toga.

some expression in a speech made by Tiberius, Atteius Capito[257] affirmed, "that if it was not Latin, at least it would be so in time to come;" "Capito is wrong," cried Marcellus; "it is certainly in your power, Caesar, to confer the freedom of the city on whom you please, but you cannot make words for us." Asinius Gallus[258] tells us that he was formerly a pugilist, in the following epigram.

Qui caput ad laevam deicit, glossemata nobis
Praecipit; os nullum, vel potius pugilis.

Who ducked his head, to shun another's fist,
Though he expound old saws,—yet, well I wist,
With pummelled nose and face, he's but a pugilist.

---

257   See before, c. x.
258   See CLAUDIUS, c. x1i. and note.

XXIII. REMMIUS PALAEMON[259], of Vicentia[260], the offspring of a bond-woman, acquired the rudiments of learning, first as the companion of a weaver's, and then of his master's, son, at school. Being afterwards made free, he taught at Rome, where he stood highest in the rank of the grammarians; but he was so infamous for every sort of vice, that Tiberius and his successor Claudius publicly denounced him as an improper person to have the education of boys and young men entrusted to him. Still, his powers of narrative and agreeable style of speaking made him very popular; besides which, he had the gift of making extempore verses. He also wrote a great many in various and uncommon metres. His insolence was such, that he

---

259   Remmius Palaemon appears to have been cotemporary with Pliny and Quintilian, who speak highly of him.

260   Now Vicenza.

called Marcus Varro "a hog;" and bragged that "letters were born and would perish with him;" and that "his name was not introduced inadvertently in the Bucolics[261], as Virgil divined that a Palaemon would some day be the judge of all poets and poems." He also boasted, that having once fallen into the hands of robbers, they spared him on account of the celebrity his name had acquired.

He was so luxurious, that he took the bath many times in a day; nor did his means suffice for his extravagance, although his school brought him in forty thousand sesterces yearly, and he received not much less from his private estate, which he managed with great care. He also kept a broker's shop for the sale of old clothes; and it is well known that a vine[262], he planted

---

261   "Audiat haec tantum vel qui venit, ecce, Palaemon."–Eccl. iii. 50.
262   All the editions have the word vitem; but we might conjecture, from the large produce,

himself, yielded three hundred and fifty bottles of wine. But the greatest of all his vices was his unbridled licentiousness in his commerce with women, which he carried to the utmost pitch of foul indecency[263]. They tell a droll story of some one who met him in a crowd, and upon his offering to kiss him, could not escape the salute, "Master," said he, "do you want to mouth every one you meet with in a hurry?"

XXIV. MARCUS VALERIUS PROBUS, of Berytus[264], after long aspiring to the rank

---

that it is a mistake for vineam, a vineyard: in which case the word vasa might be rendered, not bottles, but casks. The amphora held about nine gallons. Pliny mentions that Remmius bought a farm near the turning on the Nomentan road, at the tenth mile-stone from Rome.

263 "Usque ad infamiam oris."–See TIBERIUS, p. 220, and the notes.

264 Now Beyrout, on the coast of Syria. It was one of the colonies founded by Julius Caesar when he transported 80,000 Roman citizens to foreign parts.–JULIUS, xlii.

of centurion, being at last tired of waiting, devoted himself to study. He had met with some old authors at a bookseller's shop in the provinces, where the memory of ancient times still lingers, and is not quite forgotten, as it is at Rome. Being anxious carefully to reperuse these, and afterwards to make acquaintance with other works of the same kind, he found himself an object of contempt, and was laughed at for his lectures, instead of their gaining him fame or profit. Still, however, he persisted in his purpose, and employed himself in correcting, illustrating, and adding notes to many works which he had collected, his labours being confined to the province of a grammarian, and nothing more. He had, properly speaking, no scholars, but some few followers. For he never taught in such a way as to maintain the character of a master; but was in the habit of admitting one or two, perhaps at most three or four, disciples in the afternoon; and while he lay at ease and chatted freely on ordinary topics, he occasionally read some book to them, but that did not often happen. He published a few slight treatises on some subtle questions, besides which, he left a large collection of observations on the language of the ancients.

Lives of Eminent Rhetoricians

I. RHETORIC, ALSO, AS WELL as Grammar, was not introduced amongst us till a late period, and with still more difficulty, inasmuch as we find that, at times, the practice of it was even prohibited. In order to leave no doubt of this, I will subjoin an ancient decree of the senate, as well as an edict of the censors:–"In the consulship of Caius Fannius Strabo, and Marcus

Palerius Messala[265]: the praetor Marcus Pomponius moved the senate, that an act be passed respecting Philosophers and Rhetoricians. In this matter, they have decreed as follows: 'It shall be lawful for M. Pomponius, the praetor, to take such measures, and make such provisions, as the good of the Republic, and the duty of his office, require, that no Philosophers or Rhetoricians be suffered at Rome.'"

After some interval, the censor Cnaeus Domitius Aenobarbus and Lucius Licinius Crassus issued the following edict upon the same subject: "It is reported to us that certain persons have instituted a new kind of discipline; that our youth resort to their schools; that they have assumed the title of Latin Rhetoricians; and that young men waste their time there for whole days together. Our ancestors have ordained what instruction it is fitting their children should receive, and what

265   This senatus consultum was made A.U.C. 592.

schools they should attend. These novelties, contrary to the customs and instructions of our ancestors, we neither approve, nor do they appear to us good. Wherefore it appears to be our duty that we should notify our judgment both to those who keep such schools, and those who are in the practice of frequenting them, that they meet our disapprobation."

However, by slow degrees, rhetoric manifested itself to be a useful and honourable study, and many persons devoted themselves to it, both as a means of defence and of acquiring reputation. Cicero declaimed in Greek until his praetorship, but afterwards, as he grew older, in Latin also; and even in the consulship of Hirtius and Pansa[266], whom he calls "his great and noble disciples." Some historians state that Cneius Pompey resumed the practice of declaiming even during the civil war, in order

---

266   Hirtius and Pansa were consuls A.U.C. 710.

to be better prepared to argue against Caius Curio, a young man of great talents, to whom the defence of Caesar was entrusted. They say, likewise, that it was not forgotten by Mark Antony, nor by Augustus, even during the war of Modena. Nero also declaimed[267] even after he became emperor, in the first year of his reign, which he had done before in public but twice. Many speeches of orators were also published. In consequence, public favour was so much attracted to the study of rhetoric, that a vast number of professors and learned men devoted themselves to it; and it flourished to such a degree, that some of them raised themselves by it to the rank of senators and the highest offices.

But the same mode of teaching was not adopted by all, nor, indeed, did individuals always confine themselves to the same system, but each varied his plan of teaching according to circumstances. For they were

---

267   See NERO, c. x.

accustomed, in stating their argument with the utmost clearness, to use figures and apologies, to put cases, as circumstances required, and to relate facts, sometimes briefly and succinctly, and, at other times, more at large and with greater feeling. Nor did they omit, on occasion, to resort to translations from the Greek, and to expatiate in the praise, or to launch their censures on the faults, of illustrious men. They also dealt with matters connected with every-day life, pointing out such as are useful and necessary, and such as are hurtful and needless. They had occasion often to support the authority of fabulous accounts, and to detract from that of historical narratives, which sort the Greeks call "Propositions," "Refutations" and "Corroboration," until by a gradual process they have exhausted these topics, and arrive at the gist of the argument.

Among the ancients, subjects of controversy were drawn either from history, as indeed some are even now, or from actual facts, of recent occurrence. It was, therefore, the custom to state them precisely, with details of the names of places. We certainly so find them collected and published, and it may be well to give one or two of them literally, by way of example:

"A company of young men from the city, having made an excursion to Ostia in the summer season, and going down to the beach, fell in with some fishermen who were casting their nets in the sea. Having bargained with them for the haul, whatever it might turn out to be, for a certain sum, they paid down the money. They waited a long time while the nets were being drawn, and when at last they were dragged on shore, there was no fish in them, but some gold sewn up in a basket. The buyers claim the haul as theirs, the fishermen assert that it belongs to them."

Again: "Some dealers having to land from

a ship at Brundusium a cargo of slaves, among which there was a handsome boy of great value, they, in order to deceive the collectors of the customs, smuggled him ashore in the dress of a freeborn youth, with the bullum[268] hung about his neck. The fraud easily escaped detection. They proceed to Rome; the affair becomes the subject of judicial inquiry; it is alleged that the boy was entitled to his freedom, because his master had voluntarily treated him as free."

Formerly, they called these by a Greek term, syntaxeis, but of late "controversies;" but they may be either fictitious cases, or those which come under trial in the courts. Of the eminent professors of this science, of whom any memorials are extant, it would not be easy to find many others than those of whom I shall now proceed to give an account.

---

268   As to the Bullum, see before, JULIUS, c. lxxxiv.

II. LUCIUS PLOTIUS GALLUS. Of him Marcus Tullius Cicero thus writes to Marcus Titinnius[269]: "I remember well that when we were boys, one Lucius Plotius first began to teach Latin; and as great numbers flocked to his school, so that all who were most devoted to study were eager to take lessons from him, it was a great trouble to me that I too was not allowed to do so. I was prevented, however, by the decided opinion of men of the greatest learning, who considered that it was best to cultivate the genius by the study of Greek." This same Gallus, for he lived to a great age, was pointed at by M. Caelius, in a speech which he was forced to make in his own cause, as having supplied his accuser, Atracinus[270], with materials for his

---

269   This extract given by Suetonius is all we know of any epistle addressed by Cicero to Marcus Titinnius.

270   See Cicero's Oration, pro Caelio, where Atracinus is frequently mentioned, especially cc. i. and iii.

charge. Suppressing his name, he says that such a rhetorician was like barley bread[271] compared to a wheaten loaf,–windy, chaffy, and coarse.

III. LUCIUS OCTACILIUS PILITUS is said to have been a slave, and, according to the old custom, chained to the door like a watch-dog[272]; until, having been presented with his freedom for his genius and devotion to learning, he drew up for his patron the act of accusation in a cause he was prosecuting. After that, becoming a professor of rhetoric, he gave instructions to Cneius Pompey the Great, and composed an account of his actions, as well as of those of his father, being the first freedman, according to the

---

271   "Hordearium rhetorem."
272   From the manner in which Suetonius speaks of the old custom of chaining one of the lowest slaves to the outer gate, to supply the place of a watch-dog, it would appear to have been disused in his time.

opinion of Cornelius Nepos[273], who ventured to write history, which before his time had not been done by any one who was not of the highest ranks in society.

IV. About this time, EPIDIUS[274] having fallen into disgrace for bringing a false accusation, opened a school of instruction, in which he taught, among others, Mark Antony and Augustus. On one occasion Caius Canutius jeered them for presuming to belong to the party of the consul Isauricus[275] in his administration of the republic; upon which he replied, that he would rather be

---

273   The work in which Cornelius Nepos made this statement is lost.

274   Pliny mentions with approbation C. Epidius, who wrote some treatises in which trees are represented as speaking; and the period in which he flourished, agrees with that assigned to the rhetorician here named by Suetonius. Plin. xvii. 25.

275   Isauricus was consul with Julius Caesar II., A.U.C. 705, and again with L. Antony, A.U.C. 712.

the disciple of Isauricus, than of Epidius, the false accuser. This Epidius claimed to be descended from Epidius Nuncio, who, as ancient traditions assert, fell into the fountain of the river Sarnus[276] when the streams were overflown, and not being afterwards found, was reckoned among the number of the gods.

V. SEXTUS CLODIUS, a native of Sicily, a professor both of Greek and Latin eloquence, had bad eyes and a facetious tongue. It was a saying of his, that he lost a pair of eyes from his intimacy with Mark Antony, the triumvir[277]. Of his wife, Fulvia, when there was a swelling in one of her cheeks, he said that "she tempted the point of his style;"[278]

---

276   A river in the ancient Campania, now called the Sarno, which discharges itself into the bay of Naples.

277   Epidius attributes the injury received by his eyes to the corrupt habits he contracted in the society of M. Antony.

278   The direct allusion is to the "style" or

nor did Antony think any the worse of him for the joke, but quite enjoyed it; and soon afterwards, when Antony was consul[279], he even made him a large grant of land, which Cicero charges him with in his Philippics[280]. "You patronize," he said, "a master of the schools for the sake of his buffoonery, and make a rhetorician one of your pot-companions; allowing him to cut his jokes on any one he pleased; a witty man, no doubt, but it was an easy matter to say smart things of such as you and your companions. But listen, Conscript Fathers, while I tell you what reward was given to this rhetorician, and let the wounds of the republic be laid bare to view. You assigned two thousand acres of the Leontine territory[281] to Sextus Clodius,

---

probe used by surgeons in opening tumours.

279   Mark Antony was consul with Julius Caesar, A.U.C. 709. See before, JULIUS, c. lxxix.

280   Philipp. xi. 17.

281   Leontium, now called Lentini, was a town

the rhetorician, and not content with that, exonerated the estate from all taxes. Hear this, and learn from the extravagance of the grant, how little wisdom is displayed in your acts."

VI. CAIUS ALBUTIUS SILUS, of Novara[282], while, in the execution of the office of edile in his native place, he was sitting for the administration of justice, was dragged by the feet from the tribunal by some persons against whom he was pronouncing a decree. In great indignation at this usage, he made straight for the gate of the town, and proceeded to Rome. There he was admitted to fellowship, and lodged, with Plancus the orator[283], whose practice it was, before he

---

in Sicily, the foundation of which is related by Thucydides, vi. p. 412. Polybius describes the Leontine fields as the most fertile part of Sicily. Polyb. vii. 1. And see Cicero, contra Verrem, iii. 46, 47.

282   Novara, a town of the Milanese.

283   St. Jerom in Chron. Euseb. describes

made a speech in public, to set up some one to take the contrary side in the argument. The office was undertaken by Albutius with such success, that he silenced Plancus, who did not venture to put himself in competition with him. This bringing him into notice, he collected an audience of his own, and it was his custom to open the question proposed for debate, sitting; but as he warmed with the subject, he stood up, and made his peroration in that posture. His declamations were of different kinds; sometimes brilliant and polished, at others, that they might not be thought to savour too much of the schools, he curtailed them of all ornament, and used only familiar phrases. He also pleaded causes, but rarely, being employed in such as were of the highest importance, and in every case undertaking the peroration only.

Lucius Munatius Plancus as the disciple of Cicero, and a celebrated orator. He founded Lyons during the time he governed that part of the Roman provinces in Gaul.

In the end, he gave up practising in the forum, partly from shame, partly from fear. For, in a certain trial before the court of the One Hundred[284], having lashed the defendant as a man void of natural affection for his parents, he called upon him by a bold figure of speech, "to swear by the ashes of his father and mother which lay unburied;" his adversary taking him up for the suggestion, and the judges frowning upon it, he lost his cause, and was much blamed. At another time, on a trial for murder at Milan, before Lucius Piso, the proconsul, having to defend the culprit, he worked himself up to such a pitch of vehemence, that in a crowded court, who loudly applauded him, notwithstanding all the efforts of the lictor to maintain order, he broke out into a lamentation on the miserable state of Italy[285], then in danger of being again

---

284   See AUGUSTUS, c. xxxvi.
285   He meant to speak of Cisalpine Gaul, which, though geographically a part of Italy, did not till a late period enjoy the privileges of

reduced, he said, into the form of a province, and turning to the statue of Marcus Brutus, which stood in the Forum, he invoked him as "the founder and vindicator of the liberties of the people." For this he narrowly escaped a prosecution. Suffering, at an advanced period of life, from an ulcerated tumour, he returned to Novara, and calling the people together in a public assembly, addressed them in a set speech, of considerable length, explaining the reasons which induced him to put an end to existence: and this he did by abstaining from food.

END OF THE LIVES OF GRAMMARIAN AND RHETORICIANS.

---

the other territories united to Rome, and was administered by a praetor under the forms of a dependent province. It was admitted to equal rights by the triumvirs, after the death of Julius Caesar. Albutius intimated that those rights were now in danger.

Lives of the Poets

THE LIFE OF TERENCE

PUBLIUS TERENTIUS AFER, a native of Carthage, was a slave, at Rome, of the senator Terentius Lucanus, who, struck by his abilities and handsome person, gave him not only a liberal education in his youth, but his freedom when he arrived at years of maturity. Some say that he was a captive taken in war, but this, as Fenestella[286] informs

---

286   Lucius Fenestella, an historical writer, is mentioned by Lactantius, Seneca, and Pliny,

us, could by no means have been the case, since both his birth and death took place in the interval between the termination of the second Punic war and the commencement of the third[287]; nor, even supposing that he had been taken prisoner by the Numidian or Getulian tribes, could he have fallen into the hands of a Roman general, as there was no commercial intercourse between the Italians and Africans until after the fall of Carthage[288]. Terence lived in great familiarity with many persons of high station, and especially with Scipio Africanus, and Caius Delius, whose favour he is even supposed to have purchased by the foulest means. But

---

who says, that he died towards the close of the reign of Tiberius.

287   The second Punic war ended A.U.C. 552, and the third began A.U.C. 605. Terence was probably born about 560.

288   Carthage was laid in ruins A.U.C. 606 or 607, six hundred and sixty seven years after its foundation.

Fenestella reverses the charge, contending that Terence was older than either of them. Cornelius Nepos, however, informs us that they were all of nearly equal age; and Porcias intimates a suspicion of this criminal commerce in the following passage:–

"While Terence plays the wanton with the great, and recommends himself to them by the meretricious ornaments of his person; while, with greedy ears, he drinks in the divine melody of Africanus's voice; while he thinks of being a constant guest at the table of Furius, and the handsome Laelius; while he thinks that he is fondly loved by them, and often invited to Albanum for his youthful beauty, he finds himself stripped of his property, and reduced to the lowest state of indigence. Then, withdrawing from the world, he betook himself to Greece, where he met his end, dying at Strymphalos, a town in Arcadia. What availed him the friendship of Scipio, of Laelius, or of Furius, three of the most affluent nobles of that age? They did not even minister to his necessities so much as to provide him a hired house, to which his slave might return with the intelligence of his master's death."

He wrote comedies, the earliest of which, The Andria, having to be performed at the public spectacles given by the aediles[289], he was commanded to read it first before Caecilius[290]. Having been introduced while Caecilius was at supper, and being meanly dressed, he is reported to have read the beginning of the play seated on a low stool near the great man's couch. But after reciting

---

289   These entertainments were given by the aediles M. Fulvius Nobilior and M. Acilius Glabrio, A.U.C. 587.

290   St. Jerom also states that Terence read the "Andria" to Caecilius who was a comic poet at Rome; but it is clearly an anachronism, as he died two years before this period. It is proposed, therefore, to amend the text by substituting Acilius, the aedile; a correction recommended by all the circumstances, and approved by Pitiscus and Ernesti.

a few verses, he was invited to take his place at table, and, having supped with his host, went through the rest to his great delight. This play and five others were received by the public with similar applause, although Volcatius, in his enumeration of them, says that "The Hecyra[291] must not be reckoned among these."

The Eunuch was even acted twice the same day[292], and earned more money than any comedy, whoever was the writer, had ever done before, namely, eight thousand sesterces[293]; besides which, a certain sum accrued to the author for the title. But Varro

---

291   The "Hecyra," The Mother-in-law, is one of Terence's plays.

292   The "Eunuch" was not brought out till five years after the Andria, A.U.C. 592.

293   About 80 pounds sterling; the price paid for the two performances. What further right of authorship is meant by the words following, is not very clear.

prefers the opening of The Adelphi[294] to that of Menander. It is very commonly reported that Terence was assisted in his works by Laelius and Scipio[295], with whom he lived in such great intimacy. He gave some currency to this report himself, nor did he ever attempt to defend himself against it, except in a light way; as in the prologue to The Adelphi:

Nam quod isti dicunt malevoli, homines nohiles
Hunc adjutare, assidueque una scribere;
Quod illi maledictun vehemens existimant,

---

294   The "Adelphi" was first acted A.U.C. 593.

295   This report is mentioned by Cicero (Ad Attic, vii. 3), who applies it to the younger Laelius. The Scipio here mentioned is Scipio Africanus, who was at this time about twenty-one years of age.

Eam laudem hic ducit maximam: cum
  illis placet,
Qui vobis universis et populo placent;
Quorum opera in bello, in otio, in
  negotio,
Suo quisque tempore usus est sine
  superbia.

———For this,
Which malice tells that certain noble
  persons
Assist the bard, and write in concert
  with him,
That which they deem a heavy slander,
  he
Esteems his greatest praise: that he
  can please
Those who in war, in peace, as
  counsellors,
Have rendered you the dearest services,
And ever borne their faculties so
  meekly.
Colman.

He appears to have protested against this imputation with less earnestness, because the notion was far from being disagreeable to Laelius and Scipio. It therefore gained ground, and prevailed in after-times.

Quintus Memmius, in his speech in his own defence, says "Publius Africanus, who borrowed from Terence a character which he had acted in private, brought it on the stage in his name." Nepos tells us he found in some book that C. Laelius, when he was on some occasion at Puteoli, on the calends [the first] of March,[296] being requested by his wife to rise early, begged her not to suffer him to be disturbed, as he had gone to bed late, having been engaged in writing with more than usual success. On her asking him to tell her what he had been writing, he repeated the verses which are found in the Heautontimoroumenos:

---

296   The calends of March was the festival of married women. See before, VESPASIAN, c. xix.

Satis pol proterve me Syri promessa–
Heauton. IV. iv. 1.
I'faith! the rogue Syrus's impudent
pretences–

Santra[297] is of opinion that if Terence required any assistance in his compositions[298], he would not have had recourse to Scipio and Laelius, who were then very young men, but rather to Sulpicius

---

297   Santra, who wrote biographies of celebrated characters, is mentioned as "a man of learning," by St. Jerom, in his preface to the book on the Ecclesiastical Writers.

298   The idea seems to have prevailed that Terence, originally an African slave, could not have attained that purity of style in Latin composition which is found in his plays, without some assistance. The style of Phaedrus, however; who was a slave from Thrace, and lived in the reign of Tiberius, is equally pure, although no such suspicion attaches to his work.

Gallus[299], an accomplished scholar, who had been the first to introduce his plays at the games given by the consuls; or to Q. Fabius Labeo, or Marcus Popilius[300], both men of consular rank, as well as poets. It was for this reason that, in alluding to the assistance he had received, he did not speak of his coadjutors as very young men, but as persons of whose services the people had full experience in peace, in war, and in the administration of affairs.

After he had given his comedies to the world, at a time when he had not passed his thirty-fifth year, in order to avoid suspicion,

---

299   Cicero (de Clar. Orat. c. 207) gives Sulpicius Gallus a high character as a finished orator and elegant scholar. He was consul when the Andria was first produced.

300   Labeo and Popilius are also spoken of by Cicero in high terms, Ib. cc. 21 and 24. Q. Fabius Labeo was consul with M. Claudius Marcellus, A.U.C. 570 and Popilius with L. Postumius Albinus, A.U.C. 580.

as he found others publishing their works under his name, or else to make himself acquainted with the modes of life and habits of the Greeks, for the purpose of exhibiting them in his plays, he withdrew from home, to which he never returned. Volcatius gives this account of his death:

**Sed ut Afer sei populo dedit comoedias,
Iter hic in Asiam fecit. Navem cum semel
Conscendit, visus nunquam est. Sic vita vacat.**

**When Afer had produced six plays for
the entertainment of the people,
He embarked for Asia; but from the time
he went on board ship
He was never seen again. Thus he
ended his life.**

Q. Consentius reports that he perished at sea on his voyage back from Greece, and that one hundred and eight plays, of which he had made a version from Menander[301], were lost with him. Others say that he died at Stymphalos, in Arcadia, or in Leucadia, during the consulship of Cn. Cornelius Dolabella and Marcus Fulvius Nobilior[302], worn out with a severe illness, and with grief and regret for the loss of his baggage, which he had sent forward in a ship that was wrecked, and contained the last new plays he had written.

In person, Terence is reported to have been rather short and slender, with a dark complexion. He had an only daughter, who

---

301 The story of Terence's having converted into Latin plays this large number of Menander's Greek comedies, is beyond all probability, considering the age at which he died, and other circumstances. Indeed, Menander never wrote so many as are here stated.

302 They were consuls A.U.C. 594. Terence was, therefore, thirty-four years old at the time of his death.

was afterwards married to a Roman knight; and he left also twenty acres of garden ground[303], on the Appian Way, at the Villa of Mars. I, therefore, wonder the more how Porcius could have written the verses,

——nihil Publius
Scipio profuit, nihil et Laelius, nihil
Furius,
Tres per idem tempus qui agitabant
nobiles facillime.
Eorum ille opera ne domum quidem
habuit conductitiam

---

303   Hortulorum, in the plural number. This term, often found in Roman authors, not inaptly describes the vast number of little inclosures, consisting of vineyards, orchards of fig-trees, peaches, etc., with patches of tillage, in which maize, legumes, melons, pumpkins, and other vegetables are cultivated for sale, still found on small properties, in the south of Europe, particularly in the neighbourhood of towns.

Saltem ut esset, quo referret obitum domini servulus.[304]

Afranius places him at the head of all the comic writers, declaring, in his Compitalia,

Terentio non similem dices quempiam.
Terence's equal cannot soon be found.

On the other hand, Volcatius reckons him inferior not only to Naevius, Plautus, and Caecilius, but also to Licinius. Cicero pays him this high compliment, in his Limo—

Tu quoque, qui solus lecto sermone, Terenti,
Conversum expressumque Latina voce Menandrum
In medio populi sedatis vocibus offers,

---

304   Suetonius has quoted these lines in the earlier part of his Life of Terence. See before p. 532, where they are translated.

Quidquid come loquens, ac omnia dulcia dicens.

"You, only, Terence, translated into Latin, and clothed in choice language the plays of Menander, and brought them before the public, who, in crowded audiences, hung upon hushed applause—

Grace marked each line, and every period charmed."

So also Caius Caesar:

Tu quoque tu in summis, O dimidiate Menander,
Poneris, et merito, puri sermonis amator,
Lenibus atque utinam scriptis adjuncta foret vis
Comica, ut aequato virtus polleret honore

THE LIFE OF JUVENAL

**Cum Graecis, neque in hoc despectus parte jaceres!
Unum hoc maceror, et doleo tibi deesse, Terenti.**

"You, too, who divide your honours with Menander, will take your place among poets of the highest order, and justly too, such is the purity of your style. Would only that to your graceful diction was added more comic force, that your works might equal in merit the Greek masterpieces, and your inferiority in this particular should not expose you to censure. This is my only regret; in this, Terence, I grieve to say you are wanting."

THE LIFE OF JUVENAL

D. JUNIUS JUVENALIS, who was either the son[305] of a wealthy freedman, or

---

305   Juvenal was born at Aquinum, a town of the Volscians, as appears by an ancient MS., and is intimated by himself. Sat. iii. 319.

brought up by him, it is not known which, declaimed till the middle of life[306], more from the bent of his inclination, than from any desire to prepare himself either for the schools or the forum. But having composed a short satire[307], which was clever enough, on Paris[308], the actor of pantomimes, and also on the poet of Claudius Nero, who was puffed up by having held some

––––––––––

306   He must have been therefore nearly forty years old at this time, as he lived to be eighty.

307   The seventh of Juvenal's Satires.

308   This Paris does not appear to have been the favourite of Nero, who was put to death by that prince (see NERO, c. liv.) but another person of the same name, who was patronised by the emperor Domitian. The name of the poet joined with him is not known. Salmatius thinks it was Statius Pompilius, who sold to Paris, the actor, the play of Agave;

Esurit, intactam

Paridi nisi vendat Agaven.

–Juv. Sat. vii. 87.

inferior military rank for six months only; he afterwards devoted himself with much zeal to that style of writing. For a while indeed, he had not the courage to read them even to a small circle of auditors, but it was not long before he recited his satires to crowded audiences, and with entire success; and this he did twice or thrice, inserting new lines among those which he had originally composed.

**Quod non dant proceres, dabit histrio,
    tu Camerinos,
Et Bareas, tu nobilium magna atria
    curas.
Praefectos Pelopea facit, Philomela
    tribunos.**

**Behold an actor's patronage affords
A surer means of rising than a lord's!
And wilt thou still the Camerino's[309]**

309   Sulpicius Camerinus had been proconsul in Africa; Bareas Soranus in Asia. Tacit. Annal.

**court,
Or to the halls of Bareas resort,
When tribunes Pelopea can create
And Philomela praefects, who shall
rule the state?**[310]

At that time the player was in high favour at court, and many of those who fawned upon him were daily raised to posts of honour. Juvenal therefore incurred the suspicion of having covertly satirized occurrences which were then passing, and, although eighty years old

---

xiii. 52; xvi. 23. Both of them are said to have been corrupt in their administration; and the satirist introduces their names as examples of the rich and noble, whose influence was less than that of favourite actors, or whose avarice prevented them from becoming the patrons of poets.

310   The "Pelopea," was a tragedy founded on the story of the daughter of Thyestes; the "Philomela," a tragedy on the fate of Itys, whose remains were served to his father at a banquet by Philomela and her sister Progne.

at that time[311], he was immediately removed from the city, being sent into honourable banishment as praefect of a cohort, which was under orders to proceed to a station at the extreme frontier of Egypt[312]. That sort of punishment was selected, as it appeared severe enough for an offence which was venial, and a mere piece of drollery. However, he died very soon afterwards, worn down by grief, and weary of his life.

THE LIFE OF PERSIUS

AULUS PERSIUS FLACCUS was born the day before the Nones of December [4th Dec.][313], in the consulship of Fabius

---

311   This was in the time of Adrian. Juvenal, who wrote first in the reigns of Domitian and Trajan, composed his last Satire but one in the third year of Adrian, A.U.C. 872.

312   Syene is meant, the frontier station of the imperial troops in that quarter of the world.

313   A.U.C. 786, A.D. 34.

Persicus and L. Vitellius. He died on the eighth of the calends of December [24th Nov.][314] in the consulship of Rubrius Marius and Asinius Gallus. Though born at Volterra, in Etruria, he was a Roman knight, allied both by blood and marriage to persons of the highest rank[315]. He ended his days at an estate he had at the eighth milestone on the Appian Way. His father, Flaccus, who died when he was barely six years old, left him under the care of guardians, and his

314   A.U.C. 814, A.D. 62.

315   Persius was one of the few men of rank and affluence among the Romans, who acquired distinction as writers; the greater part of them having been freedmen, as appears not only from these lives of the poets, but from our author's notices of the grammarians and rhetoricians. A Caius Persius is mentioned with distinction by Livy in the second Punic war, Hist. xxvi. 39; and another of the same name by Cicero, de Orat. ii. 6, and by Pliny; but whether the poet was descended from either of them, we have no means of ascertaining.

mother, Fulvia Silenna, who afterwards married Fusius, a Roman knight, buried him also in a very few years. Persius Flaccus pursued his studies at Volterra till he was twelve years old, and then continued them at Rome, under Remmius Palaemon, the grammarian, and Verginius Flaccus, the rhetorician. Arriving at the age of twenty-one, he formed a friendship with Annaeus Cornutus[316], which lasted through life; and from him he learned the rudiments of philosophy. Among his earliest friends were Caesius Bassus[317], and Calpurnius Statura; the latter of whom died while Persius himself was yet in his youth. Servilius Numanus[318],

---

316   Persius addressed his fifth satire to Annaeus Cornutus. He was a native of Leptis, in Africa, and lived at Rome in the time of Nero, by whom he was banished.

317   Caesius Bassus, a lyric poet, flourished during the reigns of Nero and Galba. Persius dedicated his sixth Satire to him.

318   "Numanus." It should be Servilius

he reverenced as a father. Through Cornutus he was introduced to Annaeus, as well as to Lucan, who was of his own age, and also a disciple of Cornutus. At that time Cornutus was a tragic writer; he belonged to the sect of the Stoics, and left behind him some philosophical works. Lucan was so delighted with the writings of Persius Flaccus, that he could scarcely refrain from giving loud tokens of applause while the author was reciting them, and declared that they had the true spirit of poetry. It was late before Persius made the acquaintance of Seneca, and then he was not much struck with his natural endowments. At the house of Cornutus he enjoyed the society of two very learned and excellent men, who were then zealously devoting themselves to philosophical enquiries, namely, Claudius Agaternus, a physician from Lacedaemon, and Petronius Aristocrates, of Magnesia,

---

Nonianus, who is mentioned by Pliny, xxviii. 2, and xxxvii. 6.

men whom he held in the highest esteem, and with whom he vied in their studies, as they were of his own age, being younger than Cornutus. During nearly the last ten years of his life he was much beloved by Thraseas, so that he sometimes travelled abroad in his company; and his cousin Arria was married to him.

Persius was remarkable for gentle manners, for a modesty amounting to bashfulness, a handsome form, and an attachment to his mother, sister, and aunt, which was most exemplary. He was frugal and chaste. He left his mother and sister twenty thousand sesterces, requesting his mother, in a written codicil, to present to Cornutus, as some say, one hundred sesterces, or as others, twenty pounds of wrought silver[319], besides about seven hundred books, which, indeed, included

319   Commentators are not agreed about these sums, the text varying both in the manuscripts and editions.

his whole library. Cornutus, however, would only take the books, and gave up the legacy to the sisters, whom his brother had constituted his heirs.

He wrote[320] seldom, and not very fast; even the work we possess he left incomplete. Some verses are wanting at the end of the book[321], but Cornutus thoughtlessly recited it, as if it was finished; and on Caesius Bassus requesting to be allowed to publish it, he delivered it to him for that purpose., In his younger days, Persius had written a play, as well as an Itinerary, with several copies of verses on Thraseas' father-in-law, and Arria's[322] mother, who had made

---

320   See Dr. Thomson's remarks on Persius, before, p. 398.

321   There is no appearance of any want of finish in the sixth Satire of Persius, as it has come down to us; but it has been conjectured that it was followed by another, which was left imperfect.

322   There were two Arrias, mother and

away with herself before her husband. But Cornutus used his whole influence with the mother of Persius to prevail upon her to destroy these compositions. As soon as his book of Satires was published, all the world began to admire it, and were eager to buy it up. He died of a disease in the stomach, in the thirtieth year of his age[323]. But no sooner had he left school and his masters, than he set to work with great vehemence to compose satires, from having read the tenth book of Lucilius; and made the beginning of that book his model; presently launching his invectives all around with so little scruple, that he did not spare cotemporary poets and orators, and even lashed Nero himself, who was then the reigning prince. The verse ran as follows:

---

daughter, Tacit. Annal. xvi. 34. 3.

323   Persius died about nine days before he completed his twenty-ninth year.

Auriculas asini Mida rex habet;
King Midas has an ass's ears;

but Cornutus altered it thus;

Auriculas asini quis non hahet?
Who has not an ass's ears?

in order that it might not be supposed that it was meant to apply to Nero.

THE LIFE OF HORACE

HORATIUS FLACCUS was a native of Venusium[324], his father having been, by his own account, a freedman and collector

---

324   Venusium stood on the confines of the Apulian, Lucanian, and Samnite territories. Sequor hunc, Lucanus an Appulus anceps; Nam Venusinus arat finem sub utrumque colonus.
Hor Sat. xi. 1. 34. (Sat. i. 6. 45.)

of taxes, but, as it is generally believed, a dealer in salted provisions; for some one with whom Horace had a quarrel, jeered him, by saying; "How often have I seen your father wiping his nose with his fist?" In the battle of Philippi, he served as a military tribune[325], which post he filled at the instance of Marcus Brutus[326], the general; and having obtained a pardon, on the overthrow of his party, he purchased the office of scribe to a quaestor. Afterwards insinuating himself first, into the good graces of Mecaenas, and then of Augustus, he secured no small share in the regard of both. And first, how much Mecaenas loved him may be seen by the epigram in which he says:

---

325   Horace mentions his being in this battle, and does not scruple to admit that he made rather a precipitate retreat, "relicta non bene parmula."–Ode xi. 7-9.

326   See Ode xi. 7. 1.

Ni te visceribus meis, Horati,
Plus jam diligo, Titium sodalem,
Ginno tu videas strigosiorem.[327]

But it was more strongly exhibited by Augustus, in a short sentence uttered in his last moments: "Be as mindful of Horatius Flaccus as you are of me!" Augustus offered to appoint him his secretary, signifying his wishes to Mecaenas in a letter to the following effect: "Hitherto I have been able to write my own epistles to friends; but now I am too much occupied, and in an infirm state of health. I wish, therefore, to deprive you of our Horace: let him leave, therefore, your luxurious table and come

---

327   The editors of Suetonius give different versions of this epigram. It seems to allude to some passing occurrence, and in its present form the sense is to this effect: "If I love you not, Horace, to my very heart's core, may you see the priest of the college of Titus leaner than his mule."

to the palace, and he shall assist me in writing my letters." And upon his refusing to accept the office, he neither exhibited the smallest displeasure, nor ceased to heap upon him tokens of his regard. Letters of his are extant, from which I will make some short extracts to establish this: "Use your influence over me with the same freedom as you would do if we were living together as friends. In so doing you will be perfectly right, and guilty of no impropriety; for I could wish that our intercourse should be on that footing, if your health admitted of it." And again: "How I hold you in memory you may learn from our friend Septimius[328], for I happened to mention you when he was present. And if you are so proud as to scorn my friendship, that is no reason why I should lightly esteem yours, in return." Besides this, among other drolleries, he often called

---

328   Probably the Septimius to whom Horace addressed the ode beginning

Septimi, Gades aditure mecum.–Ode xl. b. i.

him, "his most immaculate penis," and "his charming little man," and loaded him from time to time with proofs of his munificence. He admired his works so much, and was so convinced of their enduring fame, that he directed him to compose the Secular Poem, as well as that on the victory of his stepsons Tiberius and Drusus over the Vindelici[329]; and for this purpose urged him to add, after a long interval, a fourth book of Odes to the former three. After reading his "Sermones," in which he found no mention of himself, he complained in these terms: "You must know that I am very angry with you, because in most of your works of this description you do not choose to address yourself to me. Are you afraid that, in times to come, your reputation will suffer; in case it should appear that you lived on terms of intimate friendship with me?" And he wrung from him the eulogy which begins with,

---

329   See AUGUSTUS, c. xxi.; and Horace, Ode iv, 4.

THE LIFE OF HORACE

Cum tot sustineas, et tanta negotia
    solus:
Res Italas armis tuteris, moribus ornes,
Legibus emendes: in publica commoda
    peccem,
Si longo sermone morer tua tempora,
    Caesar.–Epist. ii. i.

While you alone sustain the important
    weight

Of Rome's affairs, so various and so
    great;
While you the public weal with arms
    defend,
Adorn with morals, and with laws
    amend;
Shall not the tedious letter prove a
    crime,
That steals one moment of our Caesar's
    time.–Francis.

In person, Horace was short and fat, as

he is described by himself in his Satires[330], and by Augustus in the following letter: "Dionysius has brought me your small volume, which, little as it is, not to blame you for that, I shall judge favourably. You seem to me, however, to be afraid lest your volumes should be bigger than yourself. But if you are short in stature, you are corpulent enough. You may, therefore, if you will, write in a quart, when the size of your volume is as large round as your paunch."

It is reported that he was immoderately addicted to venery. [For he is said to have had obscene pictures so disposed in a bedchamber lined with mirrors, that, whichever way he looked, lascivious images might present themselves to his view.][331]

---

330   See Epist. i. iv. xv.

Me pinguem et nitidum bene curata cute vises.

331   It is satisfactory to find that the best commentators consider the words between brackets as an interpolation in the work of

He lived for the most part in the retirement of his farm[332], on the confines of the Sabine and Tiburtine territories, and his house is shewn in the neighbourhood of a little wood not far from Tibur. Some Elegies ascribed to him, and a prose Epistle apparently written to commend himself to Mecaenas, have been handed down to us; but I believe that neither of them are genuine works of his; for the Elegies are commonplace, and the Epistle is wanting in perspicuity, a fault which cannot be imputed to his style. He was born

---

Suetonius. Some, including Bentley, reject the preceding sentence also.

332   The works of Horace abound with references to his Sabine farm which must be familiar to many readers. Some remains are still shewn, consisting of a ruined wall and a tesselated pavement in a vineyard, about eight miles from Tivoli, which are supposed, with reason, to mark its site. At least, the features of the neighbouring country, as often sketched by the poet–and they are very beautiful–cannot be mistaken.

on the sixth of the ides of December [27th December], in the consulship of Lucius Cotta[333] and Lucius Torquatus; and died on the fifth of the calends of December [27th November], in the consulship of Caius Marcius Censorinus and Caius Asinius Gallus[334]; having completed his fifty-ninth year. He made a nuncupatory will, declaring Augustus his heir, not being able, from the

---

333   Aurelius Cotta and L. Manlius Torquatus were consuls A.U.C. 688. The genial Horace, in speaking of his old wine, agrees with Suetonius in fixing the date of his own birth:

O nata mecum consule Manlio Testa.–Ode iii. 21.

And again,

Tu vina, Torquato, move Consule pressa meo.– Epod. xiii. 8.
334   A.U.C. 745. So that Horace was in his fifty-seventh, not his fifty-ninth year, at the time of his death.

violence of his disorder, to sign one in due form. He was interred and lies buried on the skirts of the Esquiline Hill, near the tomb of Mecaenas.[335]

M. ANNAEUS LUCANUS, a native of Corduba[336], first tried the powers of his genius in an encomium on Nero, at the Quinquennial games. He afterwards recited his poem on the Civil War carried on between Pompey and Caesar. His vanity was so immense, and he gave such liberty to his tongue, that in some preface, comparing his age and his first efforts with those of Virgil, he had the assurance to say: "And

---

335   It may be concluded that Horace died at Rome, under the hospitable roof of his patron Mecaenas, whose villa and gardens stood on the Esquiline hill; which had formerly been the burial ground of the lower classes; but, as he tells us, Nunc licet Esquiliis habitare salubribus, atque Aggere in aprico spatiare.–Sat. i. 8.

336   Cordova. Lucan was the son of Annaeus Mella, Seneca's brother.

what now remains for me is to deal with a gnat." In his early youth, after being long informed of the sort of life his father led in the country, in consequence of an unhappy marriage[337], he was recalled from Athens by Nero, who admitted him into the circle of his friends, and even gave him the honour of the quaestorship; but he did not long remain in favour. Smarting at this, and having publicly stated that Nero had withdrawn, all of a sudden, without communicating with the senate, and without any other motive than his own recreation, after this he did not cease to assail the emperor both with foul words and with acts which are still notorious. So that on one occasion, when easing his bowels in the common privy, there being a louder explosion than usual, he gave vent to the nemistych of Nero: "One would suppose it was thundering under ground," in the hearing of those who were sitting there

---

337　This sentence is very obscure, and Ernesti considers the text to be imperfect.

for the same purpose, and who took to their heels in much consternation[338]. In a poem also, which was in every one's hands, he severely lashed both the emperor and his most powerful adherents.

At length, he became nearly the most active leader in Piso's conspiracy[339]; and while he dwelt without reserve in many quarters on the glory of those who dipped their hands in the blood of tyrants, he launched out into open threats of violence, and carried them so far as to boast that he would cast the emperor's head at the feet of his neighbours. When, however, the plot was discovered, he did not exhibit any firmness of mind. A confession was wrung from him without much difficulty; and, humbling himself to the most abject

---

338 They had good reason to know that, ridiculous as the tyrant made himself, it was not safe to incur even the suspicion of being parties to a jest upon him.
339 See NERO, c. xxxvi.

entreaties, he even named his innocent mother as one of the conspirators[340]; hoping that his want of natural affection would give him favour in the eyes of a parricidal prince. Having obtained permission to choose his mode of death[341], he wrote notes to his father, containing corrections of some of his verses, and, having made a full meal, allowed a physician to open the veins in his arm[342]. I have also heard it

---

340   St. Jerom (Chron. Euseb.) places Lucan's death in the tenth year of Nero's reign, corresponding with A.U.C. 817. This opportunity is taken of correcting an error in the press, p. 342, respecting the date of Nero's accession. It should be A.U.C. 807, A.D. 55.

341   These circumstances are not mentioned by some other writers. See Dr. Thomson's account of Lucan, before, p. 347, where it is said that he died with philosophical firmness.

342   We find it stated ib. p. 396, that Lucan expired while pronouncing some verses from his own Pharsalia: for which we have the authority of Tacitus, Annal. xv. 20. 1. Lucan, it

said that his poems were offered for sale, and commented upon, not only with care and diligence, but also in a trifling way.[343]

THE LIFE OF PLINY[344]

appears, employed his last hours in revising his poems; on the contrary, Virgil, we are told, when his death was imminent, renewed his directions that the Aeneid should be committed to the flames.

343   The text of the concluding sentence of Lucan's life is corrupt, and neither of the modes proposed for correcting it make the sense intended very clear.

344   Although this brief memoir of Pliny is inserted in all the editions of Suetonius, it was unquestionably not written by him. The author, whoever he was, has confounded the two Plinys, the uncle and nephew, into which error Suetonius could not have fallen, as he lived on intimate terms with the younger Pliny; nor can it be supposed that he would have composed the memoir of his illustrious friend in so

PLINIUS SECUNDUS, a native of New Como[345], having served in the wars with strict attention to his duties, in the rank of a knight, distinguished himself, also, by the great integrity with which he administered the high functions of procurator for a long period in the several provinces intrusted to his charge. But still he devoted so much attention to literary pursuits, that it would

---

cursory a manner. Scaliger and other learned men consider that the life of Pliny, attributed to Suetonius, was composed more than four centuries after that historian's death.

345   See JULIUS, c. xxviii. Caius Plinius Caecilius Secundus (the younger Pliny) was born at Como, A.U.C. 814; A.D. 62. His father's name was Lucius Caecilius, also of Como, who married Plinia, the sister of Caius Plinius Secundus, supposed to have been a native of Verona, the author of the Natural History, and by this marriage the uncle of Pliny the Younger. It was the nephew who enjoyed the confidence of the emperors Nerva and Trajan, and was the author of the celebrated Letters.

not have been an easy matter for a person who enjoyed entire leisure to have written more than he did. He comprised, in twenty volumes, an account of all the various wars carried on in successive periods with the German tribes. Besides this, he wrote a Natural History, which extended to seven books. He fell a victim to the calamitous event which occurred in Campania. For, having the command of the fleet at Misenum, when Vesuvius was throwing up a fiery eruption, he put to sea with his gallies for the purpose of exploring the causes of the phenomenon close on the spot[346]. But being prevented by contrary winds from sailing back, he was suffocated in the dense cloud of dust and ashes. Some, however, think that he was

---

346   The first eruption of Mount Vesuvius occurred A.U.C. 831, A.D. 79. See TITUS, c. viii. The younger Pliny was with his uncle at Misenum at the time, and has left an account of his disastrous enterprise in one of his letters, Epist. vi. xvi.

killed by his slave, having implored him to put an end to his sufferings, when he was reduced to the last extremity by the fervent heat.[347]

THE END OF
LIVES OF THE POETS.

---

347   For further accounts of the elder Pliny, see the Epistles of his nephew, B. iii. 5; vi. 16. 20; and Dr. Thomson's remarks before, pp. 475-478.

GRANDTYPECLASSICS.COM

"There is no friend as loyal as a book." E. Hemingway

A Christmas Carol BY C. DICKENS
A Tale of Two Cities BY C. DICKENS
Alice in Wonderland BY L. CARROLL
Animal Farm BY G. ORWELL
Anna Karenina BY L. TOLSTOY
Anne of Green Gables BY L. M. MONTGOMERY
Black Beauty BY A. SEWELL
Frankenstein BY M. SHELLEY
Gone with the Wind BY M. MITCHELL
Great Expectations BY C. DICKENS
Grimm's Fairy Tales BY J. AND W. GRIMM
In Our Time BY E. HEMINGWAY
Jane Eyre BY C. BRONTË
Les Misérables BY V. HUGO
Little Women BY L. M. ALCOTT
Moby Dick BY H. MELVILLE
Oliver Twist BY C.DICKENS
Peter Pan BY J. M. BARRIE
Pride & Prejudice BY J. AUSTEN
Robinson Crusoe BY D. DEFOE
The Art of War BY S. TZU
The Count of Monte Cristo BY A. DUMAS
And Many More...

www.ingramcontent.com/pod-product-compliance
Lightning Source LLC
Chambersburg PA
CBHW020446100426

42812CB00036B/3469/J